"An excellent resource for y—
to engage in key discipleshi—
accessible with good use of—
engage a wide audience, and yet it still contains plenty
of challenges and deeper thought. I'd recommend this
book to all youth workers as a potential resource for their
young people to read themselves or to discuss as a group."
**Paul Friend, Director South West Youth
Ministries**

"John Prockter has been working at the frontlines of
ministry for decades. He understands people, and he
knows how to help. This book is like an arm around the
shoulder from a wise old friend, encouraging us to step
out of the ruts we maybe didn't even know we'd fallen
into, and giving us a roadmap toward the new and
exciting dreams we never dared take hold of. What an
exciting gift!"
**Martin Saunders, Director of Innovation,
Youthscape**

"What an amazing book. A heart-warming read yet
challenging and thought provoking. John Prockter is a
man who doesn't just talk the talk but walks the walk
and this book displays that in bucket loads. It reminds
us of what it takes to live out our faith authentically in
the everyday. There were moments when I laughed and
moments when I felt profoundly confronted, there were
moments when I felt encouraged and deeply challenged.
This book will evoke a response on many levels but one
thing's for sure, you will be changed as a result."
**Grace Wheeler, Head of Evangelism, Youth For
Christ**

"*Reader be warned: John Prockter is about to sting you! Just when* Stuck In The Mud? *appears an easy read, it will challenge your socks off. John deals with issues we all recognise and then points us to Christ for the answer. But as simple as that sounds, he avoids the easy answers of the self-help manual, and calls us to true discipleship to know the authentic Christian life. I like the left-field illustrations and love the conclusions. All I've got to do now is live it!*"
Colin Piper, Executive Director,
World Evangelical Alliance Youth Commission

"*With an emphasis on practical, life-affirming action,* Stuck in the Mud? *is an excellent discipleship tool as it identifies specific places and moments where we get 'stuck' and then provides solid, biblical direction for how to get free from the things that hold us back. Essentially, this book is about freedom – offered generously and graciously by Christ. So, shake the mud from your boots and be prepared for a life-affirming journey as you read.*"
Nicky Geldard, Author of *Worthy*

"*I loved reading this book. It's raw and honest, practical and powerful, thoughtful and heartfelt. It's a book for anyone who is committed to keep holding on to Jesus in the midst of the often meandering – and sometimes perplexing – journey of faith and life.*"
Matt Summerfield, Senior Pastor, Zeo Church

STUCK
IN THE MUD?

Stories of Hope for When You're Stuck

JOHN PROCKTER

MONARCH
BOOKS

Published by
Lion Hudson Limited
Wilkinson House, Jordan Hill Business Park
Banbury Road, Oxford OX2 8DR, England
www.lionhudson.com

ISBN 978-0-85721-992-3
e-ISBN 978-0-85721-997-8

First edition 2021

Acknowledgments
Scripture quotations are taken from the Holy Bible, New Living Translation, copyright
©1996, 2004, 2015 by Tyndale House Foundation. Used by permission of Tyndale House
Publishers, Inc., Carol Stream, Illinois 60188. All rights reserved.

A catalogue record for this book is available from the British Library

Printed and bound in the United Kingdom, December 2020, LH26

Dedicated to the loving memory
of my dad, Edwin Prockter.

Years we've been pushing hard in a straight line,
Tripping, falling hard, but it's all fine,
Follow the star, and maybe we'll arrive on time.
Is this home? Is moving on your mind?
I'm not sure this is the right time,
But in the end, the angels all stand in line;
They sing.

Majesty, majesty.
You're the only king who could ever lead me.
We'll be fine if you take this heart of mine;
All I have is yours.
Take this mourning robe, and make a coat that shines,
Take this stubborn life of mine.

Is there some room – will they stand beside me?
I'm not sure you'll always find me;
You know the "me" that speaks when the darkness shines.
So when the world is gone, you might find me,
Stuck, kneeling alone, afraid of your mercy.
Only you can hear the whisper of my heart,
Proclaiming your Majesty.

Contents

Acknowledgments

The truth of anything like this is that no one is an island, and I'd like to acknowledge a few people who have helped me to make this book a reality.

First, and most important, my wife was extremely honest with me when I started writing this, and without her initial critique, this book would not have been any good. Thank you, sweetheart.

Second, I want to really thank Matt, Martin, and Colin. You gave me writing advice that will stay with me forever.

Third, I want to thank the people who helped me to shape this book. A special thank you to Mark Triggs, who helped me with the early editing and proofing process, and to Sarah; you've been absolute heroes. Thank you.

Finally, I'd like to thank Brad and Robin Ringer from Pure For God Ministries Inc (www.pureforgod.org) who gave me permission to talk about their study book, *First Love*. Brad and Robin have been mentors to my wife and me from before we were married, and I really commend their ministry to you.

Restoration

Do you know, the more I think of it, the more I'm convinced we're all playing a massive game of "stuck in the mud".

You know the game: one person is "on", and it's their job to tag you. When you're tagged, you're basically "stuck in the mud".

I remember playing this game at school. The most fun part was when you had to crawl through the legs of the people who were stuck. There was this tense mid-crawl moment where you were terrified that you were going to get caught. Of course, if you did get caught, you'd have to wait for others to come and release you. It was so ace.

This is a little embarrassing to admit, but there were a few times when I actually pretended to be stuck so that I didn't get tagged by my friends. Of course, it sounds stupid now, and it also rarely worked as a strategy. Ultimately, someone would see me try to move and demand that I stayed stuck as a penalty for cheating.

Now, think for a moment. If we're honest with ourselves, we'd admit that we're either constantly getting stuck by problems, or at the very least, spending most of our time navigating around them.

Granted, this is just how life is. But sometimes we get stuck because of the consequences of our own bad decisions or mistakes. Sometimes, for very different reasons, we might deliberately get ourselves stuck. At our most desperate, we might even refuse the help we need to get unstuck all together.

In some ways it is just far easier to ignore the mud we're stuck in. It's so much easier to just choose to make a fort around ourselves. But, how sad it would be if we were to set up life in this kind of way. How many years could we squander?

So, what's the plan here? Thankfully, the most helpful and freeing way to live life seems to be to value releasing ourselves and others from guilt and shame, and being restored to the perfection God always intended for us.

Ideally, despite many potential problems, we should be able to thrive if we understand our place in Christ. Easy peasy, right?

Forgive me; I couldn't help but smile as I wrote that. "Easy peasy" it most definitely is not. Frankly, most days I don't even understand enough about my relationship with Jesus to make sure I consistently succeed, let alone have any idea of how to handle the issues surrounding the people I love. But don't worry; this is why I've written this book.

It is not a succinct "how to" guide for being released and restored. Truthfully, I don't actually think any single book could be. All we can really do is own up to people we trust about where we're stuck, allow the reality of God to shape us, take the time to reflect on our relationship with Jesus, and allow the Holy Spirit to change us by His presence.

So this is the invitation.

Are you stuck, experiencing issues that you need release from?

Do you love someone who's struggling? Do you just need to experience some restoration in Jesus?

My prayer is that as you work your way through this book, you'll find encouragement, and something of the love of God. Restoration is central to God's plan, and I really hope you find some here.

Just a little housekeeping note. I really hope that each study inspires you. Following each section in Part I there's a moment to go DEEPER, with slightly more uncomfortable questions about where you're stuck at the moment. Don't panic – after we go a bit deeper, we can try to get some MOVEMENT, as we reflect and let the Holy Spirit speak.

PART I

STUCK

CHAPTER 1

Treasure: Struggling with Identity

Opposite my seat at the table there's a large white Ikea bookcase. Sometimes I catch myself staring blankly at it. My favourite thing about it is that there's a section with a large glass door, and in it I can see the reflection of a photo of a beautiful Cornish beach behind my head on the opposite side of the room.

You can find all sorts of things on our bookcase; I'm sure yours must be similar. For instance, there's a bowl full of rechargeable batteries with the must-have Dad tool: the "epic" battery tester. There's also an external hard drive, a glass coaster, a little box full of iPhone battery fixing accessories (you know, for when I'm feeling really accomplished). There's a sewing tin, an unmade child's Meccano kit, and a clay piggy bank in the shape of a VW Beetle, which we made on holiday in South Devon a long time ago. There's also a host of Blu-rays and DVDs that our kids are always asking about.

You know the sort of thing:

"What's *The Matrix*?"

"Are we allowed to watch *Die Hard*?"

To which I love to answer:

"By the time you'll be allowed to watch that, you won't want to."

Last, but by no means least, there's an array of books. Well, I might say *last*, but there's also a collection of other random toys, stones, and parts of things that our kids have absentmindedly left there.

The picture I'm trying to paint here might sound a little chaotic; a bookcase is, after all, supposed to be the sacred home of knowledge. In all honesty, my wife and I are pretty tidy people and we really value everything being in its place. But no matter how hard we try, there's always a little adventure going on among those shelves. Even just recently, our eldest daughter was asking me for something that had got lost.

The location of the treasure? The bookcase.

Fourteen months prior to this particular conversation, we'd been making stop-motion animation together. We'd had a wonderful time, and when we finished, I packed away the box and left a few characters out by mistake. I put the box away (as any well-organised father would) and I was quite sure she took the left-behind characters and shoved them on top of *The Lord of the Rings* books. Sure enough, fourteen months later, there they were, sat under a stray greeting card.

Isn't it strange how easily we can sometimes misplace the things we value most? Logically speaking, something small and reasonably insignificant could just be replaced, but there's often so much attached to the lost thing that in our hearts a simple trinket can be loaded with the worth of a memory, sometimes even bringing a sense of panic at the loss. We often make more mess finding something, don't we? I remember being moved to tears as a young boy, when I thought I'd lost a Sherwood Forest mug that my parents had given me. I flipped my whole bedroom upside down before I realised that I'd simply left it by the sofa in the living room.

When it comes to this kind of hunt, I can think of a few times when the act of looking for something ended up as special as the treasure itself. With our eldest daughter this is a reasonably regular thing. It's not that she's untidy; she just loves having everything on display. So, when something needs finding, although the process can be frustrating, I do still delight in the time we end up having together; and there's nothing quite like the sense of accomplishment when something's found.

In Luke 15 we find Jesus talking about lost things, and He tells three stories that link together. I'm sure you know the stories well, but if you're not familiar with them, Jesus is sat teaching people who are in desperate need of Him; He's also surrounded by people in authority who are not keen on what He stands for. The first story, the parable of the lost sheep, ends really helpfully with Jesus revealing the point that "there is more joy in heaven over one lost sinner who repents and returns to God than over ninety-nine others who are righteous and haven't strayed away!" (Luke 15:7 NLT).

Here's how all three stories unpack: there's a shepherd, a woman, and a father. The shepherd loses a sheep, the woman loses a coin, and the father loses a son.

Another way to look at it would be like this: there's a sheep, a coin, and a son, each one relentlessly pursued by someone who values them.

However you prefer to read it, there are three specific scenarios that tell us something about lost things, and something equally important about the shepherd, woman, and father in the parable playing the role of the finder.

In all three stories, the worth is attributed to the lost thing, but the onus is on the finder to reveal the real meaning of the situation. Of course, the sheep and coin weren't exactly able to express anything for themselves, but in the parable of the lost son we have a boy who can. Even so, his greatest accomplishment in the story is really only that he goes home, having got lost in the first place. He is not remembered for any meaningful achievement or virtuous behaviour but merely the act of returning to his father.

Reading these stories, I identify strongly with the boy, but it's the father whose unquestioning grace inspires me; the shepherd whose bold move excites me; the woman whose tenacity challenges me. I identify with the son, but I want to be bold like the shepherd, tenacious like the woman, and full of grace like the father.

These three stories that Jesus tells are very specific, but the themes aren't extraordinary in terms of the scriptural narrative.

> He wrestles,
> He whispers,
> He crashes through the heavens.
> He woos,
> He sings,
> His gift of grace is freely given.

When it comes to thinking about aspects of existence that God clearly enjoys, more than anything the answer would be – the hunt.

> *O Lord, you have examined my heart*
>   *and know everything about me.*
> *You know when I sit down or stand up.*
>   *You know my thoughts even when I'm far away.*
> *You see me when I travel*

and when I rest at home.
   You know everything I do.
You know what I am going to say
   even before I say it, LORD.
You go before me and follow me.
   You place your hand of blessing on my head.
Such knowledge is too wonderful for me,
   too great for me to understand!

I can never escape from your Spirit!
   I can never get away from your presence!
If I go up to heaven, you are there;
   if I go down to the grave, you are there.
If I ride the wings of the morning,
   if I dwell by the farthest oceans,
even there your hand will guide me,
   and your strength will support me.
I could ask the darkness to hide me
   and the light around me to become night –
   but even in darkness I cannot hide from you.
To you the night shines as bright as day.
   Darkness and light are the same to you.

You made all the delicate, inner parts of my body
   and knit me together in my mother's womb.
Thank you for making me so wonderfully complex!
   Your workmanship is marvellous – how well I know it.
You watched me as I was being formed in utter seclusion,
   as I was woven together in the dark of the womb.
You saw me before I was born.
   Every day of my life was recorded in your book.
Every moment was laid out
   before a single day had passed.

How precious are your thoughts about me, O God?
   They cannot be numbered.
I can't even count them;

> *they outnumber the grains of sand!*
> *And when I wake up,*
>   *You are still with me!*
> **Psalm 139:1–18 NLT**

The context of the hunt is something I want to be absolutely clear about. The delight that God expresses in drawing close to us is not linked to how stuck or broken we are. God delights in us, and in His presence we're restored.

Every Tuesday morning my team and I come together for a chapel service. We eat together, worship together, pray together, and we focus on different running themes. For our little group this is a really important hour for sharing and expressing some limited elements of what "church" is.

It has become a fun little tradition in my team to start the Tuesday morning chapel teaching programme with the phrase, "I was researching the topic for today, and I've found this on Google." It's only a little thing but it always raises a smile.

Returning to the point, even the most basic Google search about God delighting in us brings up many helpful results. For example, in Isaiah 62 we find a beautiful framework. God takes His bride, a holy city: a place for a set-apart people.

Contextually, we understand that to be the church, the bride of Christ. Not that we're individually married to Christ, but more that we encounter God as a part of His church, a wonderful place in which to grow.

> We are His people, and He is our God.
> We rest in His arms, we dwell in His love.
> We have been lost, we do fall down,
> We simply cannot win the crown.
> We rest in His arms, we dwell in His love.
> We are His people, and He is our God.

I mentioned how I enjoy spending time with our eldest child. Notice that I used the word "our". My daughter is the product of a marriage. She didn't just spring into being from me. I can't enjoy my time with her without acknowledging the delight of another.

She has a place of origin.

A place of rest.

A location.

A relationship.

A promise of security.

Somewhere to be loved.

Somewhere to be restored.

Somewhere to express what it means to be home.

When Jesus talks about searching and finding, He actually has a place set for us in an ancient framework; a promise of home. And all of this is designed by Him to come together in the most beautiful, fulfilling way.

Where could we possibly go? Fundamentally, we're designed to respond to Him, crafted to sway with the movement of the Holy Spirit, existing to be transformed into the likeness of Jesus.

We're His treasure, found in unlikely places. And He's ours.

DEEPER

Feeling stuck because you're not sure who you're supposed to be is very common. Sometimes we grow up struggling with who we are and where we belong. Sometimes we lose track of who we are because of stress and anxiety, but no matter the reason there's good news in Jesus. Fundamentally, it's absolutely essential to immerse yourself in the truth that you are in fact God's great treasure. His love is always present and available for you.

The depths of His commitment really are astounding: He reached down into our reality and set us in a place of safety.

He sent His only Son to die the death of a criminal so that we could have access to the fullness of what our eternal life should be.

You are His great treasure. But, He is also your greatest treasure, and herein lies the problem.

Until you're able to understand how precious God needs to be to you, you may not manage to get unstuck from an identity issue.

The reality, unfortunately, is that a wrong perspective of who God is to us is probably the sole reason why we struggle to thrive. This can lead us to relish a consumer mentality, where we go back time after time seeking something from God that we're not prepared to keep hold of in our everyday lives.

Coming back to the context of my daughter: as her parents, my wife and I hold the key to her identity as our child. But as the child, she holds the key to the relationship. Her identity is rooted in our love, our consistency, and our presence in her life. And her relationship with us is rooted in her appropriate response to that.

Obviously, on a human level, my wife and I aren't perfect, and so we hold responsibility for the relationship as well. But God is so utterly perfect, and so readily available, that the only possible conclusion to me struggling with my identity is that there's something I've missed, something I've got wrong, or something I'm deliberately ignoring.

The good news is that despite who I am, Jesus is able to do more than I could ask or imagine. What does that mean? Well, although I'm completely selfish, God will always be good, and He will always respond. But if I want to grow, I need to treat Him in a way that a holy, heavenly father needs to be treated – in reverence, recognising the perfection of His holiness.

Take some time to pray and reflect in the "Movement" section, but if identity is something you're really struggling with, you might want to consider going to Chapter 7 before reading any further.

Movement

Take a moment to open your heart in honesty before God.

Ask the Holy Spirit to show you more of the reality of God's holiness today. Try reading 1 Kings 19, where Elijah is reminded about the holiness of God in the most dramatic way.

CHAPTER 2

Humility: Dealing with Pride

There's a massive field by our home. We've always loved walking down to it. On a cold day you can look out and see the mist hovering over the valley by the river in the distance. On a hot day you can see the village on the other side. From our home you can even hear the steam train that rattles through the valley at speed; the screaming ho-o-o-o-ot that bounces around the valley is just incredible. It's the most beautiful place to live.

When our middle child Samuel was about two and a half, he wasn't very stable on his feet. The poor little chap spent most of the time flat on his face. Even now, six years later, there's a place in the alley by our home where he takes special care not to fall. He used to trip there nearly every day. When he wasn't falling on his face, he spent a considerable amount of time refusing to walk altogether. I can't blame him really; he was probably terrified of getting hurt, and he had such little legs.

On one particular occasion we went for a walk to the field with both kids and the dog. Our dog Hobie is probably the best animal you could ever meet. He's a grey border collie with striking blue eyes. In some ways, he's like a human trapped in a dog's body.

It was around Easter time and we'd only been walking in the field for about ten minutes, but Samuel had totally given up. We hadn't realised, but at some point he had stopped and sat down. We'd carried on walking and had got halfway up the field.

I can still picture the scene. Samuel had just flopped down on the track. Hobie was chasing about, hunting for pheasants in the crops. And the rest of us had got quite a bit further down the track.

Hobie was actually a rescue dog and we'd had him for a year at this point. The funny thing about Hobie and Samuel is that they hadn't really bonded. I think that, although we didn't let him get away with it, Hobie thought he was above Samuel in the family. Samuel was just this little toddling human that he could push past, and he had little respect for him.

When we realised what had happened, I turned around and shouted to encourage Samuel to catch us up.

"Samuel! Come on sweetheart!"

He didn't move.

I shouted again: "Come on Samuel, you can do it!"

He still didn't move.

I shouted again, this time with a bit of a threat, but he just wouldn't budge.

On the breeze I could hear that Samuel was crying, and honestly I was stumped. I didn't want to walk back to him, because I didn't want to give in to a tantrum. As his dad, I didn't want him to be upset either.

So that's where things stood. The girls had walked ahead, leaving me to deal with the boy. The dog was off hunting. And in a moment, our pleasant afternoon stroll had turned into a father–son Mexican stand-off.

Our semi-human dog chose that moment to ditch his hunt and focus on something far more important. I didn't actually hear him coming but I felt the sonic boom when he flew past me towards Samuel. He acted like he wasn't fussed with my response to the situation at all. I imagine that all he could see was an opportunity to practise being a sheep dog. I called over to the girls to watch what was happening.

My wife Louise, our eldest child Madeline, and I just watched in awe as Hobie rounded Samuel up like a sheep. He pounced, sprinted, barked, and sure enough Samuel got to his feet and started shuffling forward with a big smile on his face.

In Mark 5, Jesus is on an amazing journey with His disciples when He ends up healing three people. There's a demon-possessed man, a woman who's been bleeding for a long time, and a little girl who may have died.

I think the popular narrative with this passage is one about Jesus' power and authority over the spiritual realms, sickness, and death. These are my favourite themes too; however, in all three stories there are also massive distractions, all of which threaten to derail what Jesus is capable of doing.

Imagine how lame the stories would have been if they were about missed opportunities, due to extenuating circumstances.

The story of a legion of demons that was impossible to sort out. The story of a crowd where Jesus met... no one in particular. And my personal favourite – the story of when Jesus met some mourners. Classic.

In all three cases Jesus allows nothing to stop Him from getting to the person in need. He sets the man free, heals the woman, and restores the little girl to health. I know He's Jesus and so the bar is set really high. But I have to admit to at least two situations in recent days when I let an obstacle stop me from caring about a person. One time I even wanted the distraction to prevent the contact altogether.

This kind of attitude really isn't good enough, and honestly, if I want to see God break through in my life, and the lives of people around me, I've got to be better than that.

When I decided to write this book, I knew I had a tough job on my hands. Despite being a passionate storyteller, I'm not really a massively strong reader. I will, though, read and read and read and read, if it's for my children.

Why would that be remarkable? It's not really. I love them. If I were to unpack it, I'd have to conclude that I have no problem being childlike with my children.

In my living room there are lots of books I may never read. But in my kids' rooms there are books that open up their imagination, and I just love the response that I get from the time we spend together. I love the fun we have, and I love the messing around.

I just love the whole thing, including pretending to fall asleep at the end of the classic bedtime stories, where the main character typically:

Has a great big stretch,

a great big yawn,

and then falls, fast,

asleep.

Does that specific act of story-reading in the bedtime routine mean something because of the "activity"? No, obviously not. When we're together sharing an experience in this way, it's about the relationship. It's always significant, always intimate, always missed when time beats us, and always starts with me putting down something I think may be "important", for their sake.

> *Is there any encouragement from belonging to Christ? Any comfort from His love? Any fellowship together in the Spirit? Are your hearts tender and compassionate? Then make me truly happy by agreeing wholeheartedly with each other, loving one another, and working together with one mind and purpose.*
>
> *Don't be selfish; don't try to impress others. Be humble, thinking of others as better than yourselves. Don't look out only for your own interests, but take an interest in others, too.*
>
> *You must have the same attitude that Christ Jesus had.*
>
> *Though he was God,*
> *he did not think of equality with God*
> *as something to cling to.*
> *Instead, he gave up his divine privileges;*
> *he took the humble position of a slave*
> *and was born as a human being.*
> *When he appeared in human form,*
> *he humbled himself in obedience to God*
> *and died a criminal's death on a cross.*
>
> *Therefore, God elevated him to the place of highest honour*
> *and gave him the name above all other names,*
> *that at the name of Jesus every knee should bow,*
> *in heaven and on earth and under the earth,*
> *and every tongue declare that Jesus Christ is Lord,*
> *to the glory of God the Father.*
> **Philippians 2:1–11 NLT**

Years ago, I taught young people using a personal development tool created by a well-known author. The vision was to teach young people a set of principles for becoming more effective in their relationships with others – in learning how to work with others and respond positively to the inevitable challenges that arise within any relationship.

One of the most helpful principles is the concept of synergy. It's pretty straightforward and there's a school assembly that I do now and again to help to explain it. The framework of the assembly is simple. I begin with a group game, which creates a great sense of excitement and community in the assembly.

When the excitement of the activity dies down a bit, we discuss some elements of synergy, and then I finish by saying this:

"Everything that makes me who I am, and everything that makes you who you are – all of it is needed, and all of it is valuable.

"You have to realise that the people who surround you are absolutely linked to your success, and their success is completely linked to yours.

"You see, synergy is about the mixture of different things, which creates something new when they come together. Something greater than the individual parts.

"It begins with 'my' understanding, and how I choose to respond to the needs of others. I also choose to trust that they'll respond when I'm in need. And when there's the possibility, I'll commit to exploring exciting new opportunities, seeing people around me as partners, not as threats to my success."

In the book of Philippians, Paul is absolutely focused on the church figuring out how to experience real depth, free from the trappings of pride. And he's going to great lengths to nail it down.

Is Jesus moving in your life? Can you express His love? Are you kind? Are you prepared to humble yourself before God and listen to His purpose for you? Excellent. Now, go and express the same attitude that Christ had.

No matter what we talk about in terms of our relationships with others, we really should be concluding the same things each time. If we all look to meet the needs of others, then our needs will be met. And this is the case regardless of the situation, the family, the position, or the pay scale.

With this as our focus, we've got a real opportunity to see relationships from a heavenly perspective. You see, every interaction is significant and, regardless of the challenge, every person is someone we can serve, giving our all, in humility, and love.

DEEPER

People with anything to lose are in danger of feeling like they are stuck in a pride issue. Unfortunately, that pretty much means we're all in danger of getting stuck because of pride.

We're supposed to respond in love to people. As we become better at it, it's great to become more organised, perhaps even to the point where we might be managing other people. However, **Jesus is sovereign over all of it.** (Full stop.)

When we're in Christ, we simply must keep in focus that we're slaves to His will. In a very real way, this means that we have the rights to absolutely nothing – including none of the credit.

The good news is that surrendering to Jesus is the most strategic, most significant, most freeing thing you can do.

The bad news is that, the longer you leave acknowledging His Lordship, the harder it is to give things up.

However, if you're anything like me, "the good" and "the bad" aren't the point at all. The issue with pride is that we get stuck in the middle. Stuck at a point where we think *I'm* infinitely capable of fulfilling the purposes of *my own* creation.

And so, every day, in every situation, we simply must offer up everything we've been given, back to Jesus. For His glory alone.

Take some time to pray and reflect in the "Movement" section, but if pride is something you're really struggling with, you might want to consider going to Chapter 8 before reading any further.

Movement

Take a moment to open your heart in honesty before God.

Why not read the example of the rich young ruler in Mark 10:17–27? It's true that he doesn't like what Jesus tells him, but at least he asked the right question. In what ways can you give Him back the Lordship He's worthy of?

CHAPTER 3

Legacy: Coping with Disappointments

It was my first night as the manager of Bridgnorth Youth & Schools Project and The Bridge Youth Centre. It was a funny first night, because I was going to meet the group who had been loved and nurtured by other youth workers for years before I arrived. And on top of that, I had to figure out how to fit in with those people still present.

There was a range of young people. The ones I remember the most were the larger than life characters. One specific lad did everything he could to draw attention to himself. Throughout the first night you could hear his name being bellowed by the other leaders every couple of minutes.

Although I was the new manager, on that first night all I needed to do was meet people and ask questions. Of course, this particular lad ended up challenging me to a game of FIFA and I spent the whole session with him.

Week after week he came back to hang out, and every week he was a total nightmare. Some weeks he was really hard to handle, but he knew that the people in our centre believed in him, which was great. As time went on and people came and went, this lad was consistent; he always turned up. As he got older, although his behaviour sometimes got worse, his desire to stick around was strong, and so we helped him to volunteer with us.

Over the first few weeks of him being a volunteer on my team, it seemed to go really well. The other young people really liked him, and although some things were still a little chaotic, I was really happy to have him around.

As the weeks went on, autumn started to roll around, and this is when things got a little odd. At first it was things like sweets going missing from the tuck shop. Nothing crazy; just not quite right. Then a tool kit went missing, which was really strange.

All this time I was utterly clueless about how this could be happening. We were always present with the tuck shop, there was no unsupervised access to the storeroom, and there was no evidence that anyone was breaking in.

And that's when it hit me: someone must have figured out a way to break in without me noticing!

At this point it was only a theory, and I had absolutely no idea about who it was, or how or why this was happening. We went on high alert as leaders, and I made the decision not to involve any of the young people or volunteers, just in case one or more of them was involved.

Over the next four weeks we logged everything and counted the stock and money. We made a note of who locked up and who seemed keen to volunteer for important tasks. We purposefully left all the usual procedures for the keys and things exactly the same. And then, on one dark Tuesday night a month into our investigation, we got the major breakthrough that cracked the case.

I came downstairs after packing up the equipment and addressed the team: "Right. Who'd like to lock up tonight?"

One of my central team volunteered, took the key, and headed upstairs towards the back door. At that moment in walked my lad from the toilet.

"Hey, John. Would you like me to lock the back door?"

"No, it's fine mate; it's being done," I responded as my team member came down the stairs.

"OK... oh, hang on, I just remembered," he said, "I've actually left my bag upstairs! I'll just go and get it."

The other leader and I turned and looked at each other, having had the very same thought. The game's afoot.

At this point I should admit that in the event of a breakthrough like this, my team member and I had hatched a plan, code-named, "Scooby Doo".

You see, we'd worked out it was probable that someone was breaking in from the back door; we just didn't know how or when. But now we had something to go on.

I let this guy go and get his bag and then we all left the building, but not before checking the back door again. As we'd suspected, it was suddenly, mysteriously, unlocked.

Here we go. My trusty sidekick team member and I were so excited but didn't know what was going to happen next. We left the building for a little while, saying goodbye to everyone, and then silently let ourselves back in from different entrances. I came in through the garage with a torch; he came through the front door using the cover of night and a hood, just like a ninja.

We both tiptoed carefully through the pitch-black centre and met upstairs where we sat an equal position from the stairs and the very much unlocked back door.

We sat there for forty-five minutes giggling like children on a sleepover, not afraid one bit. We were, after all, simply planning to catch a teenager who was stealing from the tuck shop after dark.

Time was getting on and after the typical "Shall we just go home?" conversation, we caught sight of torchlight through the back door window. Finally, the handle turned, and the door opened.

To our amazement four lads walked in. Obviously, this wasn't quite what we'd expected and my heart did start thumping pretty quickly. But a plan's a plan, so we stuck to it.

In the next moment we both flicked our torches on, and before the four teenage numpties could do or say anything, I managed to get in a stinging one-liner worthy of Hollywood attention: "Evening lads!"

To be honest, we nearly wet ourselves laughing while all four boys got clean away, but that was also part of the "Scooby Doo" plan, so it was fine.

The last part of the plan was for me to call my young volunteer's mobile phone. There's no point in running after them when you can just make them come back to you at the touch of a button.

When he picked up the phone, the conversation went something like this:

Me: "Hey buddy."

Him: "Oh, hi John, what's up?"

Me: "Well, you just broke into the centre, so-o-o... I'm going to need you to come back for a chat."

Him: "What? That wasn't me! I'm at home!"

Me: "OK, cool. I'll just call the police."

Him: "… I'll be right back."

When he arrived back at the centre we had a pretty frank chat. He obviously assumed that he was going to be removed from the team, and he was right about that. But what he wasn't prepared for was what I felt the punishment for his crime should be.

Here's a boy with a difficult view of life and some questionable habits. As it turned out, all he was doing was letting his friends in to hang out, giving them sweets and fizzy drinks. What can I really do here? Ban him to teach him a lesson? Banning a young person certainly helps the group left behind but it doesn't do anything helpful for the one being removed.

What I actually did was pretty simple, but devastating at the same time. I told him that he was welcome back – but only once he'd paid back the money for what he'd taken. If that was tomorrow, then he would be allowed back tomorrow. Simple as that.

For this boy, that was too much. He had expected to be kicked out forever and he had no idea what he'd taken or what it was worth. He literally begged me to give him a figure that I thought was right, telling me how unfair I was being. He even had cash on him that he was willing to hand over. The truth was that I couldn't calculate it any more than he could – £5 or £100, neither of us had any idea. In the end I think he left more upset about not knowing how to make it right than he did about being caught, and of course he was pretty confused that he wasn't banned for life. He knew he could easily come back, but couldn't figure out how to get through the door.

A few weeks passed and I hadn't seen him. Finally, Christmas came and went, and in early February he finally got back in touch.

"I've figured it out," he said.

"Great!" I said. "What's the plan?"

"I'm going to fundraise for the centre."

And he did. If I remember right, he raised around £150. I'm so proud of that guy.

For every story like this, I do accept that ten other people could tell you fifty horror stories of things that went very wrong and couldn't be reconciled. Even in this story there are three lads with whom I didn't win, including the one who took the tool kit, although he did later return it.

In my experience, young people who are loved are much more likely to come back and get things sorted when things go wrong.

Whether people always come back or not, it's massively important that I make sure I don't let my reaction to issues undo good relationships. In short, I have to choose my response based on the kind of legacy I want to leave within people. Funnily enough, I also have to accept something else: I have no power to change people.

When we had our first child, I was absolutely certain that the way we parented her was by far the biggest determiner of her personality. I was so sure about the power of nurture that I would have argued the toss with pretty much anyone who challenged me. I was especially sure of it as Madeline started to grow into the model child. Talk about feeling smug!

Fast forward to Samuel, and I was still reasonably sure of the power of our parenting skills. However, by the time our third child turned two, I became quite certain that Louise and I had done very little to impact their personalities at all.

Madeline is well organised and a great leader.

Samuel is a kind, creative, team player.

Evelyn is creative and very single-minded.

And that, as they say, is pretty much the long and short of it. The thing I'm discovering is that the fundamentals of their personalities make them who they are, regardless of what we do as parents. The bits we can have an impact on seem to have more to do with fostering a sense of belonging and security, and providing unquestioning love and support in good times and in bad.

At work there's a girl that I've taught to be a pretty great public speaker. Although she can do it, I can't change the fact that this particular girl isn't extrovert enough to enjoy the experience. She has to speak to groups as part of her job; however, talking as someone who loves pretty much everything about standing in front of a crowd, it would be completely wrong of me to express any kind of disappointment in her. Not managing to catch the DNA needed to thrive in this context, quite literally, isn't anything she can control. You can learn a skill, but it doesn't mean it'll give you any kind of thrill or boost to use it. If anything, it'll take a lot of work to manage it, and it'll leave you exhausted afterwards.

If I'm right, then we have some important things to consider about our kids. We'll have to be sure that what we focus on in terms of moulding them is actually worth the effort – and whether it would be a good legacy to leave within them in the first place.

The truth is that I'm going to leave a legacy as a parent, whether I like it or not, and I need to be careful not to leave a legacy that's harmful.

What a shame it would be to leave a legacy of judgment about things I think are wrong with the people I'm supposed to nurture. How sad would it be if I left a legacy of guilt about what I failed to change or achieve with them. How devastating if we found that our children had experienced brokenness because of us. And what of the people I work with and minister to?

Thinking about life as a whole, there doesn't seem to be any room for me to be one way as a father and husband, and another way at work. Although I might favour one environment over another, I need to figure out how to leave a legacy of love, acceptance, security, and peace across the board. Surely the aim has to be to nurture children in a loving environment that provides everything they need to help them move forward in their lives and face their futures with confidence and hope.

> I'd like to pass a thing to you,
> to make the fullest difference,
> through the years that you'll be on the earth.
> But I'm afraid I've left a curse.
> I handed you a crown of gold,
> but in your hands it looks so cold.
> You didn't even try it on!
> And now I think I gave it wrong.
> The crown I thought I gave to you,
> was made of nothing you could use.

No one's perfect, but I have to understand that I can't afford to give in to my temper when someone lets me down. I can't wash my hands of people, and I can't inflict cruel and unusual punishments that will teach people a lesson.

The way I treat people needs to speak loudly about the kind of legacy I'm trying to leave – a legacy of love, acceptance, security, and peace.

Philip said, "Lord, show us the Father, and we will be satisfied."

Jesus replied, "Have I been with you all this time, Philip, and yet you still don't know who I am? Anyone who has seen me has seen the Father! So why are you asking me to show him to you? Don't you believe that I am in the Father and the Father is in me? The words I speak are not my own, but my Father who lives in me does his work through me. Just believe that I am in the Father and the Father is in me. Or at least believe because of the work you have seen me do.

"I tell you the truth, anyone who believes in me will do the same works I have done, and even greater works, because I am going to be with the Father. You can ask for anything in my name, and I will do it, so that the Son can bring glory to the Father. Yes, ask me for anything in my name, and I will do it!

"If you love me, obey my commandments. And I will ask the Father, and he will give you another Advocate, who will never leave you. He is the Holy Spirit, who leads into all truth. The world cannot receive him, because it isn't looking for him and doesn't recognise him. But you know him, because he lives with you now and later will be in you."

John 14:8–17 NLT

In John 14, we pick up with Jesus about to end His earthly ministry. He's shared His life with His disciples and now He's preparing to die. Crucially He's going to entrust the people He's invested in to the Holy Spirit, promising that they'll thrive all the more when He's gone. It's obvious that Jesus would do that; He is God after all. But it's too simplistic to just label Jesus' ease in handing His disciples to the Holy Spirit as obvious.

Jesus is in full swing in this passage, but He also acknowledges that, as a man, He doesn't know everything. And so it is absolutely relevant that He had to choose to accept the outright dysfunction of some of His disciples, while continuing to love and teach them and working to release them at the same time. Have you ever noticed that in the Gospels He accepts the particularly odd personality quirks? Like Peter suggesting they build some sheds, and here with Philip asking Jesus for an all-out supernatural circus act.

"Hey Jesus! Show us the Father! Come on, already!" In my head Philip sounds like he runs a pizza place in Brooklyn.

Jesus responds kindly to Philip and ignores the silly comment. Instead He deals with the heart of what's going on. This is well-trodden ground, but just imagine how much we'd roll our eyes if a leading minister or evangelist arrived to speak at an event with a team of complete idiots. We'd question how good a leader they were for sure. However, Jesus chooses to trust that the Father is doing something important. He changes their lives, and in complete security, works to release them. He quite literally leaves the healthiest legacy of all within them.

In all of this, let's remember the fundamentals. We're God's great treasure, designed to come alive when we truly make ourselves available in love for Him, and each other. This needs to be the basis for all of our relationships.

It's our absolute responsibility to continually orientate ourselves on the side of demonstrating love for the people we're given to take care of, whether they're our children, people we work with, or people we're responsible for. It is crucial that we strive to be:

- not opinionated, cruel, or unkind;
- not narrow minded or judgmental;
- not controlling or insecure;
- not playing judge or replacing God's heart;
- not lacking grace or denying restoration;
- not limiting the Holy Spirit or mocking the power of the cross.

God's grace is enough. And it's definitely enough to deal with whatever rubbish I pass on to people. However, that's no excuse to ignore the importance of my role and what I leave behind in the lives of my children, my wife, my team, my friends, and my young people. I really do have to make sure that I'm not passing defective legacy bombs that could explode in people's faces in the future.

And what about sin, repentance, and forgiveness? Surely we can treat people differently if they're not right before God?

Well, no. And I'm afraid that's not what this chapter is about. This is more about you and me. But just to be clear:

Only Jesus could deal with it.

Only the Holy Spirit could convict of it.

Only God could judge it.

Only the person could accept it.

Only the fruit could be sure of it.

Only the lifestyle could speak of it.

Only the replication could prove it.

Only the legacy could show for it.

And if your legacy is love, theirs will be too.

DEEPER

When we're talking about legacy, it's important to recognise that, for most of us, there will have been a time when we experienced the feeling that we're not getting what we want out of life. And so the idea of considering what we're leaving behind can be quite painful.

Truthfully, this is an issue because disappointments can grind us to a full stop, and often regardless of whether we have a solid sense of our identity in Christ or not.

For some, there are times when we'll look around to see that our relationships aren't working. For others, it'll just simply be that something has gone wrong. Obviously, at a personal level, both are equally devastating.

Regardless of what the problem is, it's important that we keep our focus on this simple truth: **Jesus is not, and never was here to be, a vending machine offering personal gratification.**

Disappointments will come and go, but God's faithful love endures forever. Our responsibility is to find a way to wake up each day with the resolve to serve Christ.

No leader and no disciple will ever be perfect. And even the best of us will struggle from time to time. But if you're feeling like you're not who you're supposed to be, it's definitely time to get back to the basics of your everyday walk with Jesus, remembering that we're here to worship Him.

Take some time to pray and reflect in the "Movement" section, but if discouragement is something you're really struggling with, then you might want to consider going to Chapter 9 before reading any further.

Movement

Take a moment to open your heart in honesty before God.

Have you experienced disappointments? In which ways has Jesus brought you through them?

CHAPTER 4

Worship: Not Experiencing God

I was like a lot of young Christian musicians in the mid-nineties. The only reason I ever picked up a guitar was because of Oasis, and the only reason I got into trying to lead worship was because Matt Redman and Martin Smith had released their songs with chord charts, which you could buy as A4 booklets. It was the best time. I knew what the songs sounded like because I had the tapes to listen to, and I could just keep practising those chords until I could actually play them.

My friend Ian and I would swap notes.

He would say, "Can you play F sharp minor yet?"

I'd reply, "Yeah! And I found a workaround so you don't have to play it as a bar chord!"

And he would counter, "Whoa! Look, you can do that with B too!"

Everyone's favourite song was *Over the Mountains and the Sea* by Martin Smith. We sang it, and sang it, and sang it, and harmonised beautifully on the chorus, and also danced slowly and awkwardly during the bridge. If you know the song, you'll know exactly what I'm talking about.

This one summer, though, Matt Redman blew up the scene when he played the crazy new song *I Will Dance, I Will Sing (Undignified)* at a Christian youth festival called Soul Survivor.

"Undignified" is based on the passage in 2 Samuel 6 where David is dancing before God. He's heavily criticised for it by Saul's daughter Michal. All he's doing is worshipping God; it's just that he is also half-naked and could be seen by the slaves of his servants. He was the king, so it must have been a pretty shocking moment. Still, he wasn't going to let a little embarrassment get in the way of his worship to God.

> *David retorted to Michal, "I was dancing before the LORD,*
> *who chose me above your father and all his family! He*
> *appointed me as the leader of Israel, the people of the LORD,*
> *so I celebrate before the LORD. Yes, and I am willing to look*
> *even more foolish than this, even to be humiliated in my own*
> *eyes! But those servant girls you mentioned will indeed think*
> *I am distinguished!"*
> **2 Samuel 6:21–22 NLT**

This was a powerful message to a generation of young Christians finding our identity in a church full of boring adults. We didn't understand that our parents had also danced before God in the happy-clappy eighties, and *We Want to See Jesus Lifted High* just wasn't cool any more. It was the mid-nineties and this was our time to be a much cooler dancing generation. That is, until 1997, when we would become *History Makers*, thanks again to Martin Smith and Delirious.

When I was a teenager, I went to an amazing weekly discipleship event called The Rock. It was the best, and all my Christian friends went. One of the best things about The Rock was that the worship was led by a guy who was an absolute hero of mine. He was dynamic, sensitive musically, amazing on the guitar, and his voice was just incredible. I can't remember the date, but Soul Survivor is in the summer and so it must have been at least mid-September when we were having a full-on praise party at The Rock. We'd worshipped Jesus, danced around the room, been inspired by the message, and prayed for each other before singing again.

After a while the worship leader came to the mic, having just finished a song with the band. He said, "I don't know what to do now."

I don't have the first clue what the team running The Rock thought, but in that moment he became an even bigger hero to me. He went from incredible to being truly humble as well.

Here was a worship leader who was happy to be stumped by God in the most public way. He carried on speaking: "I actually don't know where to go next. Shall we stop? Does anyone have any thoughts, or a sense of anything God might be saying?"

For everyone who has known me for a while, they know that when I was younger I really enjoyed a good heckle. I wasn't badly behaved by any stretch, but a well-placed funny comment was something I lived for.

So when this guy asked a public question to the group, I obviously had something to say.

From the middle of the crowd I shouted, "You should play *Undignified!*" In this instance I wasn't trying to be completely unhelpful; I genuinely felt that this song would be a good finale to the night.

There was just one problem. "Yes John, that would be great!" he said. "But I don't know that song."

It was at this moment that my friends turned to look at me and a little well of excitement started to churn in my stomach. This was one of the two songs I could actually play.

I can't quite remember whether it was me or my friend Simon who shouted that I knew how to play it, but within seconds the worship leader had taken off his guitar and told me to lead the song with his band.

There was something really special about The Rock. There was always a high sense of expectation of what the Holy Spirit would do. We were all completely in love with Jesus, and we were taught to be aware of each other as worshippers.

And that's how it happened. The crowd parted as I slowly made my way to take over the band. Here I was, a sixteen-year-old bedroom musician who'd only just started to sing, and I had never performed anything, ever.

I remember vividly the very next moment and the five minutes that followed it as if it happened just last night. I had no idea how to strike up a band or how to use a microphone, so I simply started playing and hoped for the best. Do keep in mind that this band was amazing, so they could read me easily. As I strummed away, they kicked in and we were off. I played and sang while everyone jumped around the room. I don't remember whether I did well or not. Maybe I didn't, but I'll choose to remember it as if I nailed it, if you don't mind. Either way, I think we can agree that the Holy Spirit loves a good party.

Just think for a moment about the great parties that you've been to. They always include people you care about, or at least people whom you're willing to be a bit foolish with.

When we're talking about sung worship we have to think in a similar way. The sung worship space should be full of people that you care about, that you're willing to be foolish with, and of course who love Jesus as much as you do. When we sing together there are so many possibilities, and there's a genuine opportunity to experience synergy. Like with King David, there are times when it'll even be untameable, and rightly so: God is also untameable!

> You're a lion in a battle,
> When my heart is full of fear,
> I'll sing to You.
> You're a rider on a white horse,
> When the dark is drawing near,
> I'll sing to You.
> And You gather me, hold me in Your hands;
> And You promise me, You will stay with me.
> Jesus, You're worthy, Your love won it all.

If sung worship is supposed to be dynamic, then it might even be the reason why there isn't a specific gifting to go with it. Sure, you need some talent. But leading sung worship isn't a "spiritual gift", as such. Maybe sung worship is simply supposed to be an outpouring of love; an environment for God to share with us while we are fully open to Him.

Think of it like this. We know how to be right before Him, because there are rules for that. However, when it comes to worship, He's given us a range of tools to use, which is great. Depending on the way we organise them, we can give glory back to Him in infinitely different and creative ways. It's perhaps not surprising then that there isn't a time when God outlines the kind of specific expressive worship He likes.

In Scripture, it's all either God delighting in us, or us delighting in Him. Of course, singing isn't always in the frame, but it has a special place. There's loads of singing throughout the Old Testament; then, when Jesus appears on earth as a man, people worship Him in different elaborate ways. But after He rises from the dead and ascends into heaven, the singing resumes. Check out Acts 16 for a great example.

If I were to draw a conclusion I'd say that sung worship has a close relationship with the outworking of our fundamental relationship with God.

In Zephaniah 3 God sings over us, and what happens? We sing right back. The love song between God and people seems to literally be the foundation of the eternal conversation; and the more we sing to each other, the more the gifts in the church are released. Exciting, right? It's not that the gifts within the church build good worship; it's gloriously the other way around!

I used to lead worship at a stately home kind of building just outside of a small town in the South West. There were times when I could see visions of heaven while I was leading. The outpouring of love in the worshippers was so wonderful, and it's undeniable that gifts were released. To be honest, I could probably write a book based on the fruit from those times of ministry alone, but there are plenty of far better qualified people who could tell you those stories.

Hindsight is a wonderful thing, and in some ways a lot of those experiences were unremarkable in and of themselves. However, these kinds of formative experiences are really important, especially when you're young and figuring out where you fit in the world.

Practically speaking, simply going through things like this is of worth, but there's also a more mystical element to it. There are places that people visit to experience the Almighty, where you could almost reach out and touch Him, and that's certainly how it felt to us as well: we were all there with one purpose; there was a high sense of expectation; we were totally in love with Jesus, and we were taught to be aware of each other.

In my opinion, this is the reason why we could feel the kingdom of heaven brush past us in that place. We were delighting in God with complete awareness of each other in the worship space; and the Holy Spirit responded in love, delighting in us, and releasing gifts. Why should it work this way? Well, I think it's simple. It's our love that ignites His heart. And it's His love that completes ours.

DEEPER

Sung worship can be a real issue for lots of us.

For some, the expressive style can definitely be uncomfortable, and the emotional engagement can be really confusing. This can be all the more difficult if you've been deeply let down or hurt by someone that you trusted.

For others, frustration can stem from feeling like you are being led in worship by someone who isn't capable of leading you into God's presence. Either way, you're well and truly stuck.

Here's the issue: **the sung worship space is not about you.** Sung worship is exclusively about giving worth back to Jesus, recognising His holiness.

So, do you find yourself sad and discouraged in sung worship? Do you find yourself thinking things like, "This worship didn't do anything for me today"? You may simply be stuck because you've missed the point.

Don't get me wrong; if you've been deeply hurt by someone, then trusting your heavenly Father can be a real issue. The solution is the same though: recognise His holiness.

King David said it best in Psalm 103 when he demanded that his soul get on with worshipping God. It may well be time for you to do the same.

Take some time to pray and reflect in the "Movement" section, but if worship is something you're really struggling with, then you might want to consider going to Chapter 10 before reading any further.

Movement

Take a moment to open your heart in honesty before God.

What is stopping you from worshipping Jesus today? Maybe you've had an argument with a friend or partner, or you've had some bad news at work that is preoccupying you. Whatever it may be, will you allow who God is to shape your response in love for Him?

CHAPTER 5

Peace: Overtaken by Stress

It was an early autumn morning and my wife and I were late for work. It was no big deal, except that we were also struggling to get a toddler ready, which made things at least three times more difficult.

We lived in a beautiful cottage with a hardwood floor in the living room and, since having Madeline, we'd put down a really nice thick rug that filled the entire space. It was the sort of cottage that always felt like Christmas, and Madeline had made all her major baby milestones in there. She even walked for the first time in that very room.

On this particular morning we'd gone through the whole breakfast routine and were nearly ready to leave the house, when I realised that Madeline didn't have any shoes on. Louise was ready, I was ready, and Madeline even had her coat on, but she wasn't wearing shoes. In a moment of panic, I did the only reasonable thing that every man knows will solve any tricky situation – I called for my wife. The conversation went as you'd expect.

Me: "We can't leave yet! Madeline isn't wearing any shoes!"

Louise: "Yes she is, I put them on her!"

Me: "She must have taken them off!"

Louise: "Little madam!"

Me: "Do you know where they are?"

Louise: "No. I didn't even know she'd taken them off!"

That wasn't getting me anywhere, so I turned to my daughter for help.

Me: "Madeline, where are your shoes?"

Madeline: "I don't want to wear my shoes."

Me: "Louise, I'm going to need some help."

For the next few minutes, I searched for her little shoes in our tiny cottage. Unsurprisingly, Madeline had put them in the washing machine with all the fridge magnets and some colouring pens. I so wanted to sort it all out, but by now we were really late, and we needed to get going. It was time for a parental double team.

For some reason, Madeline was not keen to wear these shoes, but we weren't experienced enough as parents to realise that sorting out the shoes at the destination was also an option, so we soldiered on.

Louise and I divided the jobs. I went for the "holding the toddler in the air whilst kneeling on the rug" position, and Louise went for the "slip those shoes on quickly" manoeuvre. By this point Madeline was screaming, but we needed to go and so I hoisted her up into the air.

And this is when it happened. In the very same moment that I launched Madeline up above my head, I lifted my face to smile at her. As she looked down at me, she didn't smile; instead, she scowled, took her mighty right hand, and slapped me square in the nose. She hit me so hard that my eyes instantly gushed with tears. It was like a press tap in a public toilet. And as I screamed, in a very manly tone, I held on to her for dear life.

To be fair, gravity is a constant, which creates considerable down force. Also, noses are designed to be fragile, and so no matter who hits you, you're bound to cry, right?

I've told this story multiple times to young people in assemblies and lessons. The physical comedy always gets a laugh, but the purpose of the story is to explain why I had to hold on to my firstborn as if my life depended on it.

> The moment I saw her I knew I would be:
> The most patient and loving and calm of daddies.
> And when she would scream as a baby, I knew,
> I could just grab a dummy and hold on to you.
> The moment I realised that now she had grown,
> Was the same time her will came against mine at home.
> This wasn't the fairy tale song from before,
> But a human with heart, which now means much more.

Whether you're a parent or not, first and foremost, we're all human beings and, like it or not, we all have impulses that aren't always right. I'm certainly not proud of it, but in the instant after she hit me in the face, my natural instincts kicked in. My head was telling me to throw her so that I could sort my face out, while my heart was telling me to scream at her, because I was so frustrated.

Thankfully, there was a sofa directly behind her, and so if I had thrown her she would have been fine. I didn't throw her though, so don't worry.

As my head and heart were both being completely unhelpful, I can only describe my actual response as one of resolve taking over. I froze, inhaled sharply, and gripped Madeline hard until I calmed down.

There's a lot to unpack from a story like this. The point has actually changed a few times over the years. Sometimes I talk about values after telling it; sometimes I talk about being proactive. But today, I think we need to talk about rest for your soul.

Probably the most famous "rest" passage – after the Old Testament's "He leads me by still waters" passage, and of course Elijah being treated to a five-star nap – is this passage in Matthew 11.

> Then Jesus began to denounce the towns where he had done so many of his miracles, because they hadn't repented of their sins and turned to God. "What sorrow awaits you, Korazin and Bethsaida! For if the miracles I did in you had been done in wicked Tyre and Sidon, their people would have repented of their sins long ago, clothing themselves in burlap and throwing ashes on their heads to show their remorse. I tell you, Tyre and Sidon will be better off on judgment day than you.
>
> "And you people of Capernaum, will you be honoured in heaven? No, you will go down to the place of the dead. For if the miracles I did for you had been done in wicked Sodom, it would still be here today. I tell you, even Sodom will be better off on judgment day than you."
>
> At that time Jesus prayed this prayer: "O Father, Lord of heaven and earth, thank you for hiding these things from those who think themselves wise and clever, and for revealing them to the childlike. Yes, Father, it pleased you to do it this way! My Father has entrusted everything to me. No one truly knows the Son except the Father, and no one truly knows the Father except the Son and those to whom the Son chooses to reveal him."

> *Then Jesus said, "Come to me, all of you who are weary*
> *and carry heavy burdens, and I will give you rest. Take my*
> *yoke upon you. Let me teach you, because I am humble*
> *and gentle at heart, and you will find rest for your souls.*
> *For my yoke is easy to bear, and the burden I give you is*
> *light."*
> **Matthew 11:20–30 NLT**

We pick up with Jesus in this passage just after He has sent His disciples out. He is teaching, and He launches into His famous "come to me and find rest" sermon. It's funny; we know that passage really well, but the bit before it is far less famous.

Fundamentally, it's important to understand that when Jesus is speaking about rest, He is expressing a sense of sadness about people who have missed out on the fullness of knowing Him.

I don't know if it's something you often consider, but the people Jesus was talking about were perfectly normal. This is a really simple point, but helpful to understand because it's easy to miss the obvious truth about how similar we are to people we read about in Scripture.

These people were probably living lives that either felt important, too busy, or maybe even too difficult to unravel. To be honest, coming from busy communities, they would have had a lot going on, and it's not a massive stretch to consider that they may have thought that Jesus was just another guy with a helpful message and some clever tricks.

Are you piecing this together yet? These people are *us*. They have seen too much, they are coping with work stress, their relationships are complicated, their children are being uncooperative, and they are thinking, "Yeah, it's great Jesus can do miracles, but I don't really need that in my life. What I really need is access to peace!" Well, they definitely missed out, because that is exactly what Jesus was offering.

One of my favourite assemblies is one that I do to help young people understand what Lent is all about. It's a simple message and an even more basic delivery method, but it always lands really well. Usually when I take assemblies, I tell stories and try to explain big concepts for young people to chew on. My presentation style is outgoing, and it's in that context that this assembly draws people in so much – because I don't speak at all. The assembly goes a little bit like this.

Imagine that I'm standing in a hall in front of a group of a few hundred young people. In my arms against my chest is a pile of A1-sized white cards with the script on them written in massive black letters.

As I stand in silence in front of the crowd, a loud heartbeat starts thumping over the PA. I wait a moment, letting the hall settle. I take a step forward, and then turn the whole massive deck of cards around.

Over the next few minutes I slowly drop the cards, allowing enough time for everyone in the hall to read what's written on them. Each line below represents a card, and as you read, try to imagine the sound of your own heartbeat. Breathe deeply in between each line and pause for a moment at the end to reflect on the words. This is what's written on the cards:

Lent.

It lasts for 40 days.

It ends at Easter.

Life is crazy,

stressful,

full of "stuff".

Drama!! Complicated relationships.

Everything we do has a soundtrack,

a trailer with a voiceover.

But we weren't born like that.

We started life listening

to a heartbeat.

Lent is about preparing for something new,

by having less of other things.

Jesus did this before He went out to teach, and to help.

Find some space, find some quiet,

experience life without distractions.

Experience peace.

At the end, the heartbeat sound fades and I simply smile, say thank you, and leave the stage with all the cards in a mess on the floor.

The person who helped me develop this assembly is someone who really struggles to find peace of mind. That might seem a little odd to just throw in at this point, but it is relevant. Isn't it strange that peace can be something that can be understood, in the very same mind that couldn't find it?

This isn't specifically about mental health, but if I were going to speak to that person in these pages, I'd say that there is peace to be had, and even if it's fleeting, it's still a wonderful gift.

As we draw to a close for this chapter, there are a few important things I want to keep in focus, which should help us to wrap things up.

First, life doesn't get any easier. The older I get, the more I realise that rushing around and being busy is not at all helpful. At the time that Madeline slapped me in the face, I was struggling with stress that made life feel really difficult. As a full-time professional in Christian youth work, I should have at least had a sense that Jesus had a practical answer to my problems. Instead, I just dug deeper and deeper, and honestly, getting hit in the face by my own child was pretty much the least of my problems.

Second, peace can be genuinely hard to find. The truth is that the same things that cause us to rush around often also cause considerable stress, but that doesn't make them unnecessary. It's an obvious point, but can you remember the passage where Mary and Martha meet Jesus? Mary sits and makes herself available in the moment, while Martha busily rushes around. Jesus says that Mary chose better, but He doesn't tell Martha that she's wasting her time. He knew as much as she did that what she was doing was also important. The issue was more that she didn't need to do those things at that exact moment.

So, what's the goal here?

Do I need to order my life better? Do I need to strip away some things that are filling my time? Do I need to say "no" to more things and "yes" only to what I prayerfully choose to fill my time with?

Yes. Please do all three.

It's always right to consider what's happening around you. But cast your mind back to the chapter about legacy. In the same way that you should make sure not to berate others, we also need to be kind to ourselves and remember that things won't always be perfect. You choose right one day, wrong the next. Most of the time, it's no big deal.

Last, and most important, we're designed to come alive in new and exciting ways when we surrender ourselves to Jesus. There's no other way to swing this. Life is both practical and spiritual, and this has to impact the way I cope with each day.

In Deuteronomy 1 there's a promise that we'll be carried through the wilderness. That is comforting, but as I grow I have to recognise that the one doing the carrying would actually far prefer to walk alongside me. I didn't specifically ask God about it, but I know it as a parent, and so I can be confident it's true of the divine as well.

As I respond to Jesus' teaching, and put things into practice, the more I'll grow and experience His peace. And for the times when the practicalities of life and health overtake me, I can be sure that I'm still being carried by a loving God whose heart breaks for my situation, and will never let me go.

Remember: we're still God's great treasure, designed to come alive when we truly make ourselves available in love for Him, and each other.

The availability I'm talking about isn't a choice: it's about surrender. We don't really love to surrender to anything, and losing control often doesn't feel great. But it's the feeling of losing control that stopped people responding to Jesus in Matthew 11. And it's the feeling of wanting my own control that stops me from finding the kind of peace that Jesus has to offer in my everyday life. The irony is that in Jesus, at the point of surrender, I gain every good thing back.

Of course, that feels scary from my point of view, but from a heavenly perspective, it makes perfect sense. And so, I'll surrender. And I'll let Him provide the peace.

DEEPER

So, we get stuck because we miss the truth of our identity.

We get stuck because of pride.

We get stuck because of disappointment.

And we get stuck because we're not experiencing God.

But if we suffer all of that, and we're also stuck because we're not experiencing His peace, then we will spiritually suffocate.

You see, we're not designed to be so full that we feel anxiety. That's why anxiety and stress can be so awful that they make us unwell.

And here's the difficult truth. Medical issues aside, if you're stuck because of stress, and you're feeling anxious: **you're probably deliberately ignoring Jesus' offer of peace.**

Please don't get me wrong. Life is truly hard, and some stress can actually be helpful. But if you consider the reason for your anxiety or stress, and genuinely match it up to what Jesus has to offer, you couldn't justify it with a straight face.

"I'm feeling stressed because of exams." OK. Let Jesus do His thing.

"I'm feeling anxious because of work." OK. Let Jesus do His thing.

"I'm feeling stuck because of this relationship." OK. Let Jesus take it.

This shouldn't be a surprise to you, but if it is, make sure you breathe this in deeply: he's got something you can handle, already prepared for you to hold.

Please let me be absolutely clear with you. If stress or anxiety is something you're really struggling with, you will want to consider speaking to a professional. Speaking to someone with experience is of course very important.

However, this shouldn't stop you from also taking hold of your opportunity right now to pray and reflect in the "Movement" section, because the Holy Spirit wants to give you peace.

If you'd like to take this subject on further, you might want to consider skipping to Chapter 11 before moving on.

Movement

Take a moment to open your heart in honesty before God.

Stop. Breathe this chapter in for a few moments.

What would "rest for your soul" mean to you today?

CHAPTER 6

Loss: Stuck in the Mud

My dad found it really hard to make plans. In between his lifelong need for naps, he struggled to fit in things that needed doing in the "every day", let alone having the headspace to consider something that someone else thought might be fun or important. I think that made him kind of selfish at times, but he wasn't malicious; he had just struggled with various forms of illness his entire life and had always had to work around that.

For my siblings and me, it had been difficult growing up with a dad who couldn't give us the attention we wanted, and as adults with children of our own, we had to just get on with it. In some ways, being the only son who lived far away made my time with my parents more difficult, but then it took so much effort to see them that we often managed to get the best from our visits, with fresh memories of pizza and buffets once or twice a year.

On one particular occasion, I made the decision to drive to my parents' house with a surprise picnic. My wife thought I was crazy and even the kids were telling me that Grandad Lincoln might struggle, but I was really disappointed not to see my mum on Mother's Day and this was only three or so weeks later, so it felt like an absolute win. I'd see Dad, and surprise Mum with a pre-made lunch. What could go wrong? As it happened, the plan worked great, and the time we spent with them was really memorable. I had no idea that this would be the last time I would see my dad in reasonably good health.

Unfortunately, not long after that visit he was taken ill, and my older sister and brother rang me to tell me he was dying. It was an odd, scary feeling driving to my family home to wait for my dad to die. To be honest, Dad had always thought he was dying, so I was finding it hard to believe. While I was driving, I had the car stereo tuned to Radio 4, and I listened to a fascinating discussion about space and time, which I was glued to.

The two compelling arguments in the discussion were about whether time is objectively constant, or whether it's more personally subjective. Time is basically measured by our movement in space, and so in some ways, the reality of time seems to be both objective and subjective. For example, you could walk down the street to the shop every week, and it might take you ten minutes every time, but if you were to meet someone important, or have a life-defining experience on that journey to the shop, it might take on a much deeper meaning within itself. You could have walked it a hundred times, but then, because of one experience, it might almost feel as if part of you exists in the experience: in that moment.

I'll be honest; I didn't understand much of what they were saying, but after I arrived and sat by Dad's bed, it struck me that there are moments in which I exist more and for longer than others, regardless of the actual passage of time.

For example, the birth of our first child took hours and hours; that's proved by the recorded time it took. But I'm convinced that a part of my soul exists in the sound of the FM radio that played a disco tune at one point. From my wife screaming out in pain, and me crying my heart out, right through to the final moments of joy and relief when our daughter was born, all of it seems to be contained in that one disco tune on the radio, which couldn't have lasted more than a few minutes.

The birth of our second child took even longer, but my wife's waters breaking will stay with me forever as both shocking and hilarious. I'll never forget the midwife gasping and then politely saying, "I've never seen so much water in a bir... oh my, they're still coming!"

The birth of our third child was a bit more routine, but when she came out and didn't cry, I experienced an eternity of pain, which I'll never forget. Even though she was absolutely fine, the single minute of panic was so horrible that I'm sure it will be etched on my heart forever.

While we sat in the hospital, I chuckled to myself that Dad wouldn't have coped with this. He would have left ages ago because he would have needed a break and a lie-down. He also would have left because the car park is really expensive! That was a classic Dad move.

I also couldn't stop thinking about the things that upset him. He never really got over the death of his mother, and he desperately missed his own father, but when he spoke about them both, his feelings were similar. With his own mum he just desperately wished he'd had more time with her, but he was in some ways more upset and had a deep sense of disappointment about not making the most of the time with his own dad.

Not so long ago he spoke to me about it, and in an odd moment, he cautioned me about the feelings I might have about the amount of time I had with him when he passed away. It was too difficult to explain to him at the time, but the truth is that I have no regrets when it comes to my dad. I spent some wonderful life-giving moments with him, which will stay with me forever. I'm just sad that his health prevented him from spending more time with me.

Disappointment was a big thing for him. I'll never forget how much he cried about not being able to find a restaurant he could afford for us to eat at when we were children.

He loved us all dearly, and he had a strong feeling of responsibility, which guided him. Yes, my siblings and I all felt he could have made a little more effort to have fun with us. However, with the precious little energy he had as a sickly man, he worked to complete a long working life before retiring. He then lived a life of ministry in the church in early retirement, a life of love with us, his wife and children, and finally a life chronicling his days, supporting and being supported by my mum; offering whatever else he had left to spare, which wasn't a lot.

I love my dad with all my heart, and I'm proud to carry on his legacy of responsibility in my own life.

We used to speak nearly every Sunday afternoon, and he'd tell me about his health problems, but those endless conversations pretty much leave me like blossom in the wind next to the precious time we had sharing that surprise picnic at Easter.

The picnic was the final time he saw me, my wife, and my kids, but I'm so pleased we got to spend this time together. In my heart, and I hope in my children's memories, this is where Grandad Lincoln will exist for years to come.

Do you know, that last paragraph just had me sitting for ages staring into space?

I don't know if you've thought about this before, but there are some stories which end so abruptly that they leave you feeling totally abandoned, unsure about how you're supposed to feel. For me, this makes for horrible reading because a story should invite you to be able to move on once it's over.

Great stories have an inbuilt mechanism that helps us to leave them behind. Conversely, bad story endings can leave you feeling like you're not at all ready to let go. They rob you of the kind of peace that a satisfying resolution provides.

It's for this reason that I think loss of any kind feels like getting stuck. Whether it's a child who misplaces a special gift, or an adult who suffers the most horrible bereavement, loss most certainly feels like a kind of crash. There's no other way to describe it.

When my father died, I remember just sitting in stunned silence. I had my mum and siblings around me, but my wife and kids were at home a couple of hundred miles away, and the immediate grief felt like a heavy thud, a literal stop – a bad end to what had been a good life, and a great story.

Contextually speaking, I do appreciate it's strange to talk in this kind of way about loss when the last study was about exploring the need to accept the peace of God in our lives, but there it is. When all is said and done, sometimes you just get stuck, and despite being the location of all peace, it's interesting to reflect upon how Jesus found Himself stricken with grief, and "stuck" as well.

I don't know how much you understand the Gospels, but they're quite cleverly written. Mark is accepted as the first Gospel account with only the book of James being older than it in the New Testament. It's almost as if Mark looked at James' book and decided it needed to establish Jesus as a saviour a bit more effectively. After Mark came Matthew, who basically took Mark's book, and wrote his own version specifically for Jews.

Then a little later, Luke wrote his book. He wrote like he didn't feel that Mark was detailed enough, but then finally, a good twenty years later John or a little team of disciples writing in his name, released a book that would demonstrate to new Christians the awe and wonder of Jesus as God.

In this book, we read about the brother of Mary and Martha being raised from the dead. It's a similar story to the one about Jairus' daughter in Mark, Matthew, and Luke, but John raises the stakes considerably, and he's the only one who even mentions it.

In the story of Jairus' daughter, the little girl has only just passed away when Jesus arrives, and the writers use the story as a way of showing His power. However, John seems to want to go further, with two far more essential details.

First, John points out that Jesus feels loss acutely as a human. Second, he focuses on showing us that Jesus has power, not only over whether people die or not – that's easy. He goes much further, making sure we know that He also holds power to return souls back to their bodies. This isn't merely bringing life back; this is full-on resurrection!

> When Mary arrived and saw Jesus, she fell at his feet and said, "Lord, if only you had been here, my brother would not have died."
>
> When Jesus saw her weeping and saw the other people wailing with her, a deep anger welled up within him and he was deeply troubled. "Where have you put him?" he asked them.
>
> They told him, "Lord, come and see." Then Jesus wept. The people who were standing nearby said, "See how much he loved him!" But some said, "This man healed a blind man. Couldn't he have kept Lazarus from dying?"
>
> Jesus was still angry as he arrived at the tomb, a cave with a stone rolled across its entrance. "Roll the stone aside," Jesus told them.
>
> But Martha, the dead man's sister, protested, "Lord, he has been dead for four days. The smell will be terrible."
>
> Jesus responded, "Didn't I tell you that you would see God's glory if you believe?" So, they rolled the stone aside. Then Jesus looked up to heaven and said, "Father, thank you for hearing me. You always hear me, but I said it out loud for the sake of all these people standing here, so that they will believe you sent me." Then Jesus shouted, "Lazarus, come out!" And the dead man came out, his hands and feet bound in grave-clothes, his face wrapped in a head-cloth. Jesus told them, "Unwrap him and let him go!"
>
> John 11:32–44 NLT

Let's deal with the first thing: Jesus feeling the pain of loss.

In this story, we get thirty-four verses that detail what Jesus was doing before He fully felt the pain of the loss of His friend. He's on a mission with His disciples, and He knows that Lazarus has died, but for some reason, He seems to act as if He's got all the time in the world.

I don't know for sure but I think John writes the story in this way to demonstrate Jesus showing His divinity, but in the process, he perfectly sets Jesus up for a very human emotional breakdown, which is genius.

When Jesus does finally arrive, He's confronted by Mary and comes to realise very quickly that they've buried Lazarus, which isn't what Jesus wanted. Like a poorly told story with an abrupt ending, Jesus experiences the "thud" of being stopped in His tracks, and He gets angry and upset about it.

Up until this point, He's been strong and composed, with all the power in the universe at His fingertips, but then He's met with a tomb and a friend who had been in there for four days. These details shouldn't have been a problem for Jesus, but judging by His response, they were clearly devastating.

Now let's deal with that second thing: Jesus has the power to return the soul to the body.

I think it's generally agreed that Jesus deliberately missed the death of His friend so that He could raise him back to life, but when He arrived there was still pain in the loss. Not because He couldn't deal with death, but because loss is messy and it hurts, even when you're God.

To make matters worse, Jesus was part of a culture that believed that the soul hovered over the dead body for three days before leaving altogether. So, naturally, by this point four days in, Lazarus was not just dead; he was also gone.

When Jesus comes along, He's angry that Lazarus has been put in a tomb and demands he be let out, saying that Martha should have remembered that she was going to see God's glory. Did He really expect them not to bury the decaying body of their brother? Honestly, I'm not sure, but there is so much emotion in this passage that we can conclude the writer wanted us to understand first that we can rely on the absolute power of God, and second that it's OK to allow our emotions to run their natural course.

What a privilege, to meet Jesus in His most raw moments of emotion.

As with the loss of my dad, Jesus was ultimately derailed emotionally by the finality of the situation. The story ended far too abruptly. However, if you'll allow me some more conjecture, I think we can see something important that is easily missed in the detail.

Lazarus did die.

Jesus did struggle with his death emotionally.

Jesus did raise Lazarus back to life.

And at some point, Lazarus did also die again.

When my father died, it was a shock, and getting stuck felt horrible. But in allowing God to move in that same feeling of loss, I believe that the grief was redeemed through the memories I had. The memories, in turn, began to help the pain of the loss feel more like a satisfying end to a life well lived by my dad, and that is such good news for me.

In the biblical account, Jesus raised Lazarus back to life, but we never really find out why. Lazarus doesn't join Jesus on any adventures, and he doesn't immediately start telling everyone about heaven. No – the truth seems to be far more fundamental than any of that.

I think it's possible Jesus raised Lazarus back to life just so he could end well with his family in a more satisfying and fulfilling way. Like I said, Lazarus did die again, but maybe the first time it happened quickly with no resolution. Perhaps, the second time, he died in a way that took the pain of loss and turned it into an ending that helped them all to move on.

I do appreciate that, even as I'm writing this, there's a sense of unfairness that Jesus doesn't do this kind of thing often, but I still think there's something to take away.

First, yes, God is all powerful. But more important than that, those of us left behind can rely on Jesus to understand, and join us in our loss. We can accept that He's present with us in grief, and we can allow Him to help us redeem the end of our loved one's stories in the love we have for them and the memories we shared together.

DEEPER

Death is not the end, and in some ways, our experience of life on Earth isn't really the beginning, but there is a real sense that we're called to embrace our lives with everything we have.

We know from Jeremiah that God has a plan for us to prosper in all areas of our lives; we know from Micah that we're called to walk humbly with God, and we know from John 10 that Jesus came that we would experience life in all its fullness.

There is a legitimate argument to be had about how much we're called to hold on to this life with both hands, but there's just as much to suggest that we have to hold life lightly, acknowledging the Lordship of Christ and the sovereignty of God.

When you're struggling with loss, it might just be that you're still in the middle of the mud. And on this point, you have my full support, with one caveat: **keep moving.**

Grief is a long and winding process, and the wisest people I know tell me that you never really say goodbye to it completely. However, to turn grief into a friend you're going to need to discuss it, open up about it, and learn to accept that the love you feel for the people you've said goodbye to is always going to be with you.

Be kind to yourself, and if this study has touched you, feel free to move on to Chapter 12 before continuing.

Movement

If you've experienced loss, which you're still processing, please take time to pause before moving on.

PART II

RESTORED

CHAPTER 7

Calling: Purpose and Delight

Opposite my seat at the table there's a large white Ikea bookcase. Sometimes I catch myself staring blankly at it. My favourite thing about it is that there's a section with a large glass door, and in it I can see the reflection of a photo of a beautiful Cornish beach behind my head on the opposite side of the room.

When I draw my eye line back into focus, I can see my wife sat directly opposite me wondering why I'm ignoring the storm at the table.

Directly to my right is Madeline; she's sat unusually close to me given the amount of space she has. She's rearranging her plate so that it looks like she's eaten a lot of dinner, and in the moment before I tell her off, I stop to consider whether it would be better to just let her not eat. It would certainly cause less stress.

Opposite Madeline sits Samuel. He's making fun of his mummy for a hilarious jumping tantrum she had about something the other day. Of course, I remind him that he should respect his mummy, while holding back a tiny little giggle. He's also trying his hardest to avoid eating his plate of food.

To my left at the head of the table in between Louise and me sits Evelyn. She's currently piling ketchup and mayonnaise on to her plate, and honestly, as long as she's happy I just want to leave well alone. Of course, her compliance is short-lived and she kicks off with a plate-flipping tantrum.

This is the moment that Louise notices me caught in a blissful daze. Madeline is still moving food around her plate, Evelyn has just been sent to the naughty step, and now Samuel needs me, and pipes up over the commotion.

"Daddy, can I please have another drink?" he says, like nothing just happened.

"Yes buddy, no problem," I reply. "Just be careful with the water jug."

I've no idea why, but at this point, Madeline chimes in and reaches across the table to help him. In a moment of pure chaos, Louise and I both jump up from the table. Louise goes to deal with Evelyn, and I intervene with Madeline and Samuel.

"Be careful, you two!" I growl, as Samuel races to grab the water before Madeline gets it. He reaches across the table and weaves his arm around his glass that still has a little water in it. He gets past the gravy boat, and the bread sauce, and finally gets his hand on the water jug just as Madeline grabs on too. As they both tug at it, Samuel knocks his glass with his forearm. The remainder of his water splashes all over his dinner plate in horrific slow motion.

Then, everything kicks off, with all five of us roaring in perfect unison.

Evelyn roars because she is still in the middle of a tantrum. Louise roars because Evelyn gets off the naughty step. Madeline roars at Samuel for fighting over the water. Samuel roars because his dinner is ruined, and I roar out of pure frustration. In fact, I roar in a way that breaks something in me I don't think I'll ever get back.

I bellow in such a primal growl that time itself seems to stand still – that is, except for the slow, mocking drip of the remainder of Samuel's water, falling from the table as he stands in tears.

This is not the first time and certainly wouldn't be the last that I would feel that having a sit-down meal together is sometimes far more trouble than it's worth. But despite all this, I know deep down that there is such a value to this ritual.

It is a chance to talk about what we would like to achieve together, to catch up on stories from the day and, of course, to eat. To be honest, although it's a nightmare, it is just so good for us, and a guaranteed time when we know we'll be together.

Dinner table antics aside, balancing the needs of our three children can be really tricky: each child desperately wants their own adventures with us.

Even just this weekend I had a little hike, an adventure to see a train, and a *Star Wars* gaming session, and the kids still moaned. But it's really OK. Being a husband and a father is, after all, my primary love, my main responsibility, and my calling.

My family is my world, and I would always choose them over absolutely anything else.

> If I had time to burn, I'd light the chiminea,
> And break out the marshmallows, more every year.
> When you asked me to play, I'd say yes every time,
> And I'd save time for Mummy and open more wine.
> Because you are my focus, my all every time,
> Except now and again, my work takes my time.
> Then sometimes, and often, my team have my time
> And the music I love, well, that too needs some time.
> And the house sometimes breaks,
> And the car takes my time.
> I'm still worried about money, and that needs my time.
> The extended family I love also need my time.
> And the church with the stuff going on asks for time.
> Then the growth that we all need to see takes my time.
> And now as I write there's a speed in the rhyme
> And my heart double beats because although it's mine,
> I only snatch parts
> And even that time…
> I know I don't have the first clue how to make all of this
> successful in the long term.

Right at the start of Genesis 1, God kicks off the process of creation that sets this amazing order to things:

- purpose;

- activity;

- reflection;

- delight.

I'm sure this is totally familiar to you, but stick with me. When God created, He had a solid purpose for what He was doing. He created to be in perfect relationship with that very same perfect creation. Put simply, His activity, the physical act of creation, was born out of that purpose.

Then, as things went on, He reflected on the progress, and took the time He needed to delight in it. Brilliant.

You've probably picked up by now that the purpose of this book isn't to neatly pin down every theological point. It's more about inspiration. Having that as part of the purpose, it feels completely fine to write about the act of creation in one small paragraph, breezing past massive theology with a tip of the cap.

However, if my purpose here were bigger, I would probably reflect that this current section, and most of the book, isn't actually good enough. To be honest, I'm such an inexperienced writer, I'd almost certainly get disheartened and give up. I might still.

In some ways, though, successful or not, writing this book is as good a metaphor for the process of creation as I can find. Without all four elements in consideration, I simply wouldn't have a chance of succeeding in what I'm trying to do.

First and fundamentally, I'm trying to inspire you with truth. That's my purpose, and in each of the first six studies I've tried to at least touch on some of the most fundamental truths about God and our relationship with Him.

Chapter 1: We're God's great treasure.

Chapter 2: We come alive when we express love.

Chapter 3: Our legacy should be love.

Chapter 4: Our love ignites God's heart for us.

Chapter 5: We need to be defined by Jesus' peace.

Chapter 6: Jesus joins with us when we grieve.

Second, I'm planning, and getting on with, the practical activity of writing, all the time crafting and forming ideas. This activity is chosen, and in that way, it is taking focus from my usual ministry and family time. And that's completely OK.

Third, I'm constantly reflecting on the progress. I've got to make sure I'm going in the right direction, changing things to be more effective; in particular, making sure that I'm not being too precious about things and getting input where I can.

Finally, I'm re-reading my own work – not for the sake of checking it, but because I'm enjoying myself a great deal. I'm also beginning to talk about it with other people, figuring out what to do next.

You see, God's creation process is so ingrained in the fabric of reality, that you could confidently use it to inform anything. And would you expect anything else from a process endorsed by the Almighty?

Unsurprising, then, that it's even relevant to my family mealtimes. If the purpose of our mealtimes is to gel the family together, by building good relationships and learning from each other, then a few spills and even some tears are not only OK but also completely expected.

And this is the truth. If I choose something out of a sense of purpose, then a bit of chaos in the activity has to be totally fine. The problem is that so many things in life are expected of us, and things take our time and make us feel overdone with busyness. Sometimes this makes even a little bit of chaos feel absolutely crippling. Being busy in some areas is often unavoidable; however, for what we can choose, we should make sure that all of it breathes life.

> The heavens proclaim the glory of God.
> The skies display his craftsmanship.
> Day after day they continue to speak;
> night after night they make him known.
> They speak without a sound or word;
> their voice is never heard.
> Yet their message has gone throughout the earth,
> and their words to all the world.
>
> God has made a home in the heavens for the sun.
> It bursts forth like a radiant bridegroom after his wedding.
> It rejoices like a great athlete eager to run the race.
> The sun rises at one end of the heavens
> and follows its course to the other end.
> Nothing can hide from its heat.
> **Psalm 19:1–6 NLT**

There are a lot of people who wrongly assume that, because of the nature of my work, I must always be busy. The truth is that I'm often not. Not that I don't work extremely hard – I do. But I know a lot of people who are far busier than me, and I know a lot of people who don't handle their time well at all. I admire some of these people a great deal.

I wouldn't want to single out any specific person, mostly because we can all be guilty of this sort of stuff. However, we've all been on the receiving end of the kind of behaviour that shows that someone has either been hurt by other people's busyness, or that they themselves are completely overstretched. You know the kind of thing; it even comes across in simple conversations.

"I know you're really busy, but could I just have a moment?"

"I don't have long, so please could you be quick?"

"I can't stay long; I just have this other thing to get to."

In all honesty, I feel the same about being "busy" as I do about wasps. I get that it's an inevitability at times; I just hate it and want to hit it with a shoe.

Busy is a fake kind of importance. It's a "full is good", "peaceful can't be assertive" sort of lie. But I don't want to be too melodramatic. Being "full" in activity can be purposeful and incredibly fruitful. It's just that it's often not very good for us. Often we buy into being busy easily because we love the feeling of achieving things.

The difficulty is that busy for the sake of "activity" is nothing short of crazy. Busyness completely blocks our ability to reflect, and subsequently our capacity to simply delight in things.

However, activity for the fulfilment of purpose is completely and perfectly excellent. It's like the "slingshot effect". You pull back the elastic to create some tension, and then you release it. Oh! What it must feel like to be the projectile soaring through the air.

The part of this that I think is the most difficult to balance is that the same God who delights in us also deeply inspires us to do a million things to serve Him. But He doesn't want worn-out humans: that was never the plan. Remember, He's aiming for perfection, which is why, in our chaos, He never stops drawing us to quiet.

He delights over me with singing.

He carries me out of the wilderness.

He beckons me to the mouth of the cave to whisper to me.

He lays me down to rest by still waters.

He offers peace that passes all understanding.

And God does all of that, not because He hates activity, but because, like any parent, He knows what's good for His children. He knows when to ask us about our day, and how to hear our hearts. He designed it this way, and it's glorious.

I know this couple living near me who wake up each day and ask the Holy Spirit what the plan is. Whenever I drop in, they have food ready for me like they're expecting me. I also know someone who will work in a highly strategic long-term way, with plans upon plans, ready to meet every conceivable need of the people around him.

Both that couple and my friend have the very same power to choose what to fill their time with. Both have very different passions, so their decisions will be completely different. But both have the very same God, both live full lives because of a sense of purpose, and both have the same invitation to experience Him in the quiet.

What a wonderful God we have. He drives everything forward with a clear purpose. And He promises fulfilment will be there, when I choose the right things, and let go of everything else.

Movement

Take a moment to open your heart in honesty before God.

Ask God to reveal which things you need to stop doing today. If you could stop doing one thing, what would take its place?

CHAPTER 8

Presence: Learning to Be Here

There's a massive field by our home. We've always loved walking down to it. On a cold day you can look out and see the mist hovering over the valley by the river in the distance. On a hot day you can see the village on the other side. From our home you can even hear the steam train that rattles through the valley at speed; the screaming ho-o-o-o-ot that bounces around the valley is just incredible. It's the most beautiful place to live.

On this one occasion, we walked down to the river. Samuel was nearly four and he was loving the sunshine. He was skipping, running, and smiling. This is Samuel at his very best: full of beans, so brave, and, if nothing else had given it away, we knew he was loving the spring walk because he was sticking his tongue out as he ran.

As you near the river you walk among a densely wooded area, so much so that in some places you could stay dry in the rain. At the bottom of the hill, you actually get to cross the train track itself, and if you have the timetable (or are lucky) you can time your walk to wave at the train, like the railway children.

Although this was a lovely day, it had been quite wet in previous weeks. So when we crossed the line, we made sure that the kids knew to be careful – though they were completely fine, as was the dog. The problem, as it turned out, was me.

Over the previous year, it had turned into a fun ritual for the kids to walk over a log down past the track. Even though it went over a little dry ditch, it wasn't high, so was pretty safe. Today, like most other walk days, both kids ran excitedly to the log and waited for me to help them across.

Madeline went first and did it really well, but when Samuel got on, he needed me to hold his hand. As he walked across the log, I started to edge my way down the little ditch. Samuel had this massive grin on his face and I was encouraging him along. As Samuel got closer to the edge of the log, I became more aware that where I was stood was actually really wet, and becoming more and more slippery. Still, this was such a cool thing to do, and he loved it so much, that I carried on. Before I knew it, my foot slipped in a massive pile of mud that was covered by a heap of leaves. I fell so quickly that I didn't even have time to let go of Samuel. In a flash, I was face down, covered in mud, and there, in a screaming heap, was Samuel. I got myself up, and then reached down into the mud to pull him out.

I'm sure you can imagine how bad I felt. Just imagine accidentally harming your own child! To make matters worse, we just sort of brushed him off, hoping he was OK, before we established that he had actually broken his collarbone. For the first half a minute, I was like, "Hey mate, it's OK, you're fine, no need to worry." It was only when the slightest touch set him off screaming that we realised there might be something wrong.

One of my absolute favourite gospel messages to preach is also the basis for one of my most practical, demonstration-based talks.

To be honest, I find it really hard to nail a practical demonstration, and I try to avoid them if I can – especially after the time I dissected a big fat glow stick. I can't remember exactly what the point was, but at the crucial moment in my talk, I planned to snap the stick and make it glow. I don't recommend smashing the inside of a glow stick, by the way! It starts as murky yellow and then, as it breaks, the air turns it luminous. It's basically a sealed glass test tube filled with toxic gloop.

I had put this gloop-filled test tube in an empty Chinese food container. Now I was preaching, and the moment was here. I said the crucial thing in the talk, and shook the plastic container hoping for the luminous gloop to cause a great effect. The only problem was that the tube didn't break. So I shook the container harder, but nothing happened.

This was a bit of a let-down and so, as the moment was being lost, I did the only thing I could think of. I said the crucial line once more with deeper feeling and gave the container an almighty smack against the wooden lectern.

As my hand came crashing down, the container broke into pieces, crushing the glass tube inside. Instantly, the liquid turned from the standard murky yellow to its luminous glory, but in the same moment, the glass from the tube also cut into my hand. The toxic fluid got literally all over the place – in the cut, all over my skin – and it stung so bad. All I wanted to do was sort it out, but I had ten more minutes to fill, and I hadn't landed the point yet, so I pretended it was part of the act and carried on.

I never repeated that talk again but this other talk, simply named "God reached down", is one that I preach as much as I can. The message is pretty simple: you already belong.

I use my wedding ring in the talk. This is such a perfect stage prop, not least because it's always with me. But its presence on my finger is also very much the point.

Just pretend for a moment that I'm playing the role of God. I'm playing God, and my wedding ring is playing the role... of you.

It's easy to see how important my wedding ring is to me. If you were with me, you'd see it on my finger every single day. But then, it's a wedding ring and so I wear it constantly. If I removed it, you'd see a callus that shows you where it belongs. And the inside of the ring is still perfectly shiny where it connects with me. It might seem like an odd thing to think of, but even if it were removed and taken to a far-off place, it would still be mine.

No matter where my ring is,

it speaks of deep commitment,

and it always belongs on me.

The most effective place for it to be is with me,

but it doesn't really matter,

it belongs to me.

The ring itself is shaped to fit,

I've got its mark on me as well,

it still belongs with me.

In the next part of the talk, I ask for a volunteer to come and help me. Over the course of a few minutes we bury my ring in a bowl full of fake snow and we ask another person to come and retrieve it.

The snow works like magic. To begin with, it's like powder and the ring just sits on top, but when I tip a bottle of water in, the white powder quadruples in depth. It's like a more extreme version of rice, except that it's mildly toxic and by far quicker to respond to water.

And this is where things get really cool. You see, not one human on this glorious little planet asked to be here. We were just born here, growing up in the mix with everything else on Earth. It's not fair, but that doesn't change the fact that we're here, and it doesn't change the reality that we're constantly affected by things that are wrong here.

Someone starts a war – we're affected.

Someone hurts us – we're affected.

Someone tells lies about us – we're affected.

I do something wrong – someone else is affected.

I hold a grudge – someone else is affected.

I let my temper fly – someone else is affected.

Someone talks about me behind my back; I find out and say I'm cross with them but tell a third person, who's in earshot of a fourth person – we're all affected!

A bit like my ring in a bowl full of fake snow: we're quite physically buried under the effect of grimy, horrible "stuff", and the amazing things in life are incredible, but even in those perfect situations, insecurity and anxiety can still affect us and those around us. To be absolutely frank, I can hardly resolve an argument, let alone orchestrate a plan to stop every human on the planet from suffering the effect of the presence of sin in the world. And this is where our second volunteer comes in.

"Here we are. I'm ringless but the ring is still mine. The ring is fingerless and buried deep in a bowl of snow. But it still has a place where it belongs. My finger still shows the mark where it fulfils its purpose."

At this point, I ask my second volunteer to reach down into the fake snow to retrieve my ring. This is a powerful image in and of itself, but it's the next thing that happens that is just glorious.

In the moment that the second volunteer finds and redeems the ring, they instantly become conscious that they're holding my wedding ring.

The weight of responsibility always hits them and there's an instant realisation that I'm going to need it back. It's like a magnetic force that compels them.

It's really funny. They've taken the ring from the bowl, and it's covered in this wet, sticky fluff. So what do they do? They clean it! In a moment that shows a glimpse into the atonement process, the volunteer sets my ring right again, and then gives it back.

It's a wonderful picture of Jesus' eternal role. And it makes me wonder, do you even know that there's a you-shaped mark on God?

> Eventually he came to the Samaritan village of Sychar, near the field that Jacob gave to his son Joseph. Jacob's well was there; and Jesus, tired from the long walk, sat wearily beside the well about noontime. Soon a Samaritan woman came to draw water, and Jesus said to her, "Please give me a drink." He was alone at the time because his disciples had gone into the village to buy some food.
>
> The woman was surprised, for Jews refuse to have anything to do with Samaritans. She said to Jesus, "You are a Jew, and I am a Samaritan woman. Why are you asking me for a drink?"
>
> Jesus replied, "If you only knew the gift God has for you and who you are speaking to, you would ask me, and I would give you living water."
>
> "But sir, you don't have a rope or a bucket," she said, "and this well is very deep. Where would you get this living water? And besides, do you think you're greater than our ancestor Jacob, who gave us this well? How can you offer better water than he and his sons and his animals enjoyed?"
>
> Jesus replied, "Anyone who drinks this water will soon become thirsty again. But those who drink the water I give will never be thirsty again. It becomes a fresh, bubbling spring within them, giving them eternal life."
>
> "Please, sir," the woman said, "give me this water! Then I'll never be thirsty again, and I won't have to come here to get water."
>
> "Go and get your husband," Jesus told her.

> *"I don't have a husband,"* the woman replied. Jesus said,
> *"You're right! You don't have a husband – for you have had*
> *five husbands, and you aren't even married to the man*
> *you're living with now. You certainly spoke the truth!"*
> **John 4:5–18 NLT**

When Jesus meets the Samaritan woman at the well, the impact of His presence with her completely transforms her life. With no more than a few moments, He speaks effortlessly into her past, present, and future. As the story goes on, Jesus ends up staying with the people from her village and lots of them come to believe that He is indeed the messiah.

The funny thing is that, after this story, which seems to be largely about the power of Jesus' presence, He then heals a boy without His even being there. I do appreciate that He made a deeper impact on the Samaritan woman, but if we're simply talking about outcome, then He did still do the thing that was needed remotely, and that was valid in and of itself.

All this begs the question: is it Jesus' presence in the universe, His presence in the world, or His presence in our lives that is the thing that makes the real difference?

Saul walks to Damascus, and meets a vision of the ascended Jesus. The disciples go to Emmaus, but don't realise that they're talking with the risen Jesus. Mary walks in a garden and sees the gardener, but it's the risen Jesus. The disciples are in a storm on a boat, and Jesus strolls over. A Samaritan woman goes to the well, and Jesus speaks right into her life. In the beginning was the Word, the Word was with God, and the Word was God.

This all seems to be about how Jesus' presence changes everything. And I've referenced only a few examples from the New Testament. His impact on the Old Testament is just as great, and the rest of His impact on the New is even more amazing than what I've just whistled past.

But, it's the unity of God that's the key here. And it's Jesus' role in the whole reality of God that's the point.

Do you realise that the reason we can access God is because of Jesus' presence with us? And I'm talking about the whole eternal person of Jesus.

Presence in my life.

Presence in the world.

Presence in the universe.

Presence in heaven.

Presence in the completeness of everything.

It's essential that He's woven through everything, because we need Him to be able to deal with how affected we are by the world around us.

First, we need Him to be able to access us. Second, we need Him to be able to clean us. Third, we need Him to be able to present us back to the Father. And finally, we need Him to do all of that whilst still making a personal impact. Whoa! There's a you-shaped mark on His Father.

We have a place of origin.

A place of rest.

A location.

A relationship.

A promise of security.

Somewhere to be loved.

Somewhere to be restored.

Somewhere to express what it means to be home.

I can think of loads of times when I tried to be great, or cool, or special for our children. In most of those situations I messed it up, hurt them, or missed an opportunity and ended up frustrating everyone. I can think of lots of examples of the same sort with my wife. The same goes for my friends, and the people I work with.

Take, for example, Samuel walking on the log. I knew he was really too small for that, but I wanted to be a cool dad, and what did that get us? A trip to hospital.

I try all the time to be a great dad, and so I should. But for all the stock I set in the big things, if you ask Samuel what he most enjoys, he'd say watching a film, reading a book, or playing a video game with me. He's just desperate for me to be present.

And I get it: in those situations, we're both completely engaged in something together. And we're not being distracted to do anything else.

Isn't that funny? It's not the grand walk over the log that makes the difference. It's not the technical plan for a perfect demonstration with luminous yellow gloop that lands the point. It's not the perfect demo with a ring and some fancy snow that makes the difference.

It's simply that God has already shown me that I belong, and as I learn to understand His presence with me, I need to learn how to be present with Him and the people I love.

Movement

Take a moment to open your heart in honesty before God.

Whom do I most need to be "present" with?

How would I change if I were more present with Jesus?

CHAPTER 9

Grace: The Gift of Release

It was my first night as the manager of Bridgnorth Youth & Schools Project and The Bridge Youth Centre. It was a funny first night, because I was going to meet the group who had been loved and nurtured by other youth workers for years before I arrived. And on top of that, I had to figure out how to fit in with those people still present.

This wasn't an unusual feeling for me. As I stood watching my new staff and young people buzzing around, I remember thinking about what it had felt like to arrive in my previous youth work position in Exmouth. It's strange looking back at it now, from the point of view of today, well over a decade later. But when I arrived in this youth centre it had only been around six years, although that also felt like a lifetime ago.

It was a warm spring day and I was sat in traffic on my way back from Penzance to our home in South Devon. I was in my silver work van, which could really go, and generally speaking the A30 through Cornwall was a pretty fast drive. Today there were a lot of tourists around, and I'd got stuck in the mix. Stupidly, I'd had to drive 190 miles from Bristol, almost past my own home, just to install a single computer terminal in a job centre. But that was how it went working for a courier company. Install a TV. Drop a new stock checker into New Look. Replace a computer in a job centre.

This is what I was doing with my life in 2005, but it wasn't my long-term plan. In fact, the only reason I was in that van was because I'd been made redundant from a position in the South West Youth Ministries office in Exeter. I loved that job. It was the first time I had properly worked with my best friend.

Being let go was quite tough and it felt unjust at the time, but the money had dried up for the position, and truthfully, I may not have been skilled enough to succeed at it in the first place. The biggest disappointment was that Louise and I had only been married a year. The years 2003 and 2004 had been so full of promise, but so far, in terms of work, 2005 was rubbish.

I think the issue I had was that up until this point, I'd breezed through youth ministry training, and had already been a major part of setting up two excellent rural youth work projects. Not that I deserved the credit, but I was still quite pleased with myself. And here I was, no longer doing full-time youth work, but instead driving a van. Days like this when I had a lot of time to think weren't very helpful, but looking back, I had nothing to complain about. I was married, I was working, and I could volunteer in youth ministry in my spare time. Not that I would need to volunteer for much longer.

I didn't know it as I drove home, but this was the very same day I would receive an application pack for the holy grail of youth work positions in Exmouth. It was for the manager's position of the Exmouth Initiative in Christian Education (ICE) Project.

This was a job that I'd wanted for years, and I knew all about it, so applying for it was easy. I'm not proud of this, but in some ways, I felt this job was obviously going to be mine. I'd worked hard, and I felt that I deserved it; like it was mine to inherit. I was an excellent youth worker, I was even trained by previous ICE project leaders, and I was sure that I'd make a great team leader. In retrospect, I don't know why I thought that. Leading teams was something I'd been awful at so far.

I remember the interview day vividly. It was warm and I felt that I had this post solidly in the bag. I was sat in the ICE office with two other applicants, and I was sure that I was by far the strongest. The interview itself went really well, so after I got home I waited expectantly for the call. When it came, I didn't know whether I should feel crushed, or whether I should crack open a bottle of champagne to celebrate. It certainly ended up being one of the strangest conversations I'd ever had.

It went something like this. "Hi John, we really want you to know that we liked you very much," said the ICE project chairman on the other end of the line.

"Thank you," I said, wondering whether anything good could follow a cautious greeting like that.

"I'm sorry we kept you waiting," he said, "but I'm afraid you didn't get the position."

"OK, thank you for letting me know." I tried hard to hide my disappointment.

"You should know that you did great, but one of the other applicants was far better qualified than you, and we really wanted a female leader this time."

He went on. "Unfortunately, she's taken a job elsewhere though, so…"

I really liked where this was going now. "Essentially, although you didn't officially get it, I'm calling tonight to offer you the job."

I wasn't keen on being the second choice, but I was thrilled to be offered the position, so I accepted the job right there on the phone. I did wonder why I needed to know that I was second choice though.

"There is something else you need to know, I'm afraid," he continued, in a more serious tone. "I'm very sorry to tell you that we've had a bit of an issue with the office email."

I didn't follow where he was going with this at all, but it didn't sound good. "John, I'm afraid the team you'll be leading know that you didn't get the job. Unfortunately, they know you're our second choice. They were sent an email with confidential details in it by mistake. I'm so sorry."

And so there I was, the first week of September, on my first day managing the Initiative in Christian Education, and to be quite honest, looking at that team, I felt a bit inadequate.

Another six years passed to 2011, and although that job had been a real youth work success, I'd actually been made redundant again. The now Open Door ICE Project was over for me, and the Bridgnorth Youth & Schools Project was my new challenge. Except this time, I was in a job where the stakes were even higher.

This time we had two kids in tow. This time we had moved to a place where we didn't know anyone. And this time I wouldn't just be leading a team; I'd be managing a building as well.

As I stood reflecting on what sometimes felt like a ministry life filled with lingering failures, I was brought back to reality by a member of my new team bawling at a kid who was drawing attention to himself. I called the lad over, and after we chatted for a bit, he challenged me to a game of FIFA.

The truth is that, like most of us, I like to remember the rose-tinted highlights of what came before. However, for perspective, it's important to keep the past in focus. For example, if I think about my journey through both redundancies and a host of other problems, then I have to admit that the entire reason why I didn't crash out of youth ministry is down to two significant men.

It's so funny how time works, though. During the problems, I would have credited only one of them with guiding me helpfully. You see, the other guy was the one who had made me redundant… both times! So I was quite cross with him. I just had no idea how hard he had fought for me – that is, until later. We joke, but I really love that guy.

In all honesty, I had problems before I even met him, but the other guy was consistently with me through everything. We also joke, but he's got too many embarrassing stories about me, so I generally just shower him with praise and hope for the best. You see, I probably should have been kicked out of the same training course in Devon I like to remember succeeding at in 1998. This was with Youth For Christ in the mid-Devon Connect team.

In 1999, after leaving that training placement with Connect feeling like a let-down, I became the team leader of a brand-new youth work project in Tavistock, which we named Catalyst. This was my first position as a team leader – and I was rubbish at it. Sure, I could do the youth work well, but I was also responsible for one other person, and I wasn't good at that part of the job at all. At times, I know for a fact that she hated me – although later she also married me. So, swings and roundabouts.

In the following four years I continued to do a decent job of leading people in Catalyst, and then left there – again, under a cloud.

Fast forward to around 2009, and the ICE Project I was so proud of leading was trying to get rid me. Extreme, right?

There are a lot more details that help the context here, but those are stories for another day, and I don't want to get bogged down. Suffice to say that the problem was more about personality than performance, and this is where Captain Redundancy first saved me without my knowledge.

Now, please take note, because I think this is important. The reason I'm still in ministry leadership today is because:

I was trusted by a couple of significant leaders,

guys that cared, who were very present with me.

I was constantly picked up and brushed off,

and given that crucial pep talk, ready for the next round.

I was believed in.

I was fought for.

My skills were valued,

but my bad attitudes weren't ignored.

I was invested in.

I was loved.

I was constantly released.

Importantly, I was lovingly restored.

Here I am, a numpty who didn't deserve to make it.

There's a great biblical narrative surrounding releasing and restoring people. We've touched on some of it, but there's far more to learn from it, and definitely more again than I'll be able to cover here.

Jesus constantly expresses a loving attitude towards people, releasing and restoring whomever He meets:

- a demon possessed man;
- a woman who's been bleeding for a long time;
- a little girl who may have died;
- Philip asking to see the Father;
- Peter suggesting they build a shed;
- the people of Korazin, Bethsaida and Capernaum;
- Martha, who rushed around;
- the Samaritan woman.

These are just the people I've talked about in this book so far. There's also Mary Magdalene, who anointed Jesus' feet; the crippled man who had his sin forgiven and was then miraculously healed; and the woman caught in adultery. I could go on, but perhaps I need only add Paul to the list.

Remember, this guy was a significant Jew who killed Christians. I even think he was there when Stephen was stoned. However, after Jesus appeared to him, his life was transformed, and he quite literally became the greatest human example of God's grace. More than anything, Paul was big on self-discipline.

He never seemed to stop pushing forward, and even suggested at one point that people would be better to not get married. Not that he was against marriage, but he felt that romantic love would be a real distraction when you're trying to share the gospel across the world in a short period of time. (Fair point.)

By far the most impressive thing about Paul was that he used discipline to drive his love for people being released from sin and restored in Jesus.

> *Every time I think of you, I give thanks to my God. Whenever I pray, I make my requests for all of you with joy, for you have been my partners in spreading the Good News about Christ from the time you first heard it until now. And I am certain that God, who began the good work within you, will continue his work until it is finally finished on the day when Christ Jesus returns.*
>
> *So it is right that I should feel as I do about all of you, for you have a special place in my heart. You share with me the special favour of God, both in my imprisonment and in defending and confirming the truth of the Good News. God knows how much I love you and long for you with the tender compassion of Christ Jesus.*
>
> *I pray that your love will overflow more and more, and that you will keep on growing in knowledge and understanding. For I want you to understand what really matters, so that you may live pure and blameless lives until the day of Christ's return. May you always be filled with the fruit of your salvation – the righteous character produced in your life by Jesus Christ – for this will bring much glory and praise to God.*
>
> **Philippians 1:3–11 NLT**

Before we move on, let's just make certain that we're staying on target. We're God's great treasure, which means everyone in your life is also GREAT TREASURE.

Let that sink in for a second. Even the most frustratingly different personality types to yours are also treasure, and each one of them needs to be treated as such, being held in the highest regard.

- the aim is for people to not need me any more;
- the aim is for people to graduate past my capacity;
- the aim is for people to surpass my limits;
- the aim is for my people to be the people I need to ask the big questions of;
- the truth is that people are supposed to be released;
- the truth is that people need to be restored;
- the truth is that we're designed to be who God meant us to be;
- the truth is that it's my responsibility to set people free.

Honestly, I'm no measure of success, but I've had a lot of great people speak into my life, and not one stopped me from growing, or micromanaged the joy out of me. Importantly, not one ever inflicted cruel and unusual rules to keep me in line, or squash my potential, despite my many flaws.

Again, let's connect the dots a bit. Leaving a legacy of love, hope, acceptance, and peace should be our focus, and in that way legacy, release, and restoration should have the closest of relationships.

Earlier on, when we recalled Jesus preaching after He sent out the disciples, we found Him getting on with the next important thing that He had to do with His time.

Notice that Matthew 11 isn't called "Jesus sent out His disciples, but also followed them around reprimanding them for not being excellent enough". So what actually happened?

He called His people.

He trained His people.

He released His people (despite their many flaws).

He brought them back to train them some more.

Then He released them again.

(There's something of Purpose, Activity, Reflection, and Delight in that too, isn't there?)

This is slightly off topic, but isn't it interesting how few fundamental truths there are? Right down at the very core we just keep coming back to the same basics. And here we go again.

- Understanding identity = Release.

- Love for God and each other = Release.

- Leaving a legacy of love, hope, acceptance, and peace = Release.

- Igniting God's heart with worship = Release.

- Surrendering to Jesus' peace = Release.

- Accepting God's sovereignty = Release.

- Expelling busyness = Restoration.

- Practising presence = Restoration.

- Exercising grace = Restoration.

So I'm convinced. We are all just playing a massive game of "stuck in the mud". And it's hard, isn't it? It's so much more palatable to consider external reasons why we get into trouble, but most of our problems really are of our own making. I now accept, for example, that my early youth work issues were largely because I had a dangerously inflated ego. I really struggled to see the point of loving or valuing other people.

It is, however, crucial we understand that, regardless of how or why people get stuck, our mission is to release and restore them back into the game. Really and truly, it's not hard to find people who need releasing; we're surrounded by people who get stuck in the mud, sometimes repeatedly. We've got a simple job to do in this regard: exercise God's grace.

Remember: grace is the thing you get when you don't deserve it. The other thing is called mercy. And mercy is wonderful as well, but in this case, you can't afford to be simply "merciful".

Let me explain. If I deserve a slap in the face and you don't slap me, then you've been merciful. But isn't it freeing for both of us to express true forgiveness instead? To express grace.

I might deserve a slap, but our greatest gift is to release each other from guilt and shame, seeing the potential for restoration in each other.

This is so similar to what Jesus did as He brushed me off and gave me back to the Father. And this is what exercising grace is all about. I don't deserve it, but you give it anyway, because that gift was given to you to pass on to me in the first place. And this is the ancient truth. Genesis tells us that even Adam and Eve had to be released so that they could be restored.

They did something terribly wrong – got stuck in the shame. They were released into the consequences of their sin, but only so that we could be restored through Jesus and be released from that same sin that caused their shame in the first place.

It's in this framework we can land this chapter well. First, there is an ancient truth, which makes the restoration process something we should expect for ourselves and the people around us. Second, if we're living for Jesus, then we've already been handed this legacy, and experienced God's perfect grace. Finally, our aim should be to give this same legacy to the people around us, always exercising the grace that we've been shown, as we release other people to grow.

Movement

Take a moment to open your heart in honesty before God.

Where do I most need to experience God's grace today?

Whom do I know that needs releasing today?

CHAPTER 10

Thankfulness: The Power of Understanding

I was like a lot of young Christian musicians in the mid-nineties. The only reason I ever picked up a guitar was because of Oasis, and the only reason I got into trying to lead worship was because Matt Redman and Martin Smith had released their songs with chord charts, which you could buy as A4 booklets. It was the best time. I knew what the songs sounded like because I had the tapes to listen to, and I could just keep practising those chords until I could actually play them.

There's a real sense of destiny about being a musician in my family. Although I'm not the best, I do all right, and I'm good at what I do. When I was growing up, I heard a lot of stories about my birth mum, who also played the guitar and sang. But she died when I was small, so I didn't ever get a sense of what that really meant.

My cousins' parents were musicians, and so they learnt instruments from a very young age. But the only musical legacy I was passed was a love for Kenny Rogers, ABBA, and Cliff Richard. My dad had a smart little case under his car seat, where he kept all the best driving music.

There was also a time when I tried to play the violin. I didn't really want to play it, but my big brother had just started, and I thought he was cool. It was not surprising, however, that when he lost interest in it, so did I.

I remember vividly the day that I gave up the violin – my parents were livid. My dad was especially cross with me and forbade me from playing another musical instrument ever again. He may also have sent me to my room and grounded me too. It was an extreme reaction, and I might actually be remembering some of the details wrong as I was only about nine.

When I finally caught the bug for playing guitar I was pretty insufferable. My older sister loves to recall that I would learn how to string a couple of chords together and then promptly interrupt whatever she was doing to play her my latest masterpiece. I just wanted to share my passion for music with my sister, but yeah, I was probably quite annoying. One thing is for sure: I was doing an extremely good job of not revising for my GCSEs.

As I've got older, I've found that I describe myself more and more as a leader of sung worship: a worship leader. It's true that I'm also a youth worker, but honestly, I think that standing behind a mic with my guitar is probably my most natural habitat.

One of my absolute favourite things to do is to teach worshippers and worship leaders how to grow and express themselves, the purpose being to glorify Jesus and experience change in His presence.

When I visit places where I'm asked to teach or encourage, the main barriers I find are always pretty similar. Putting aside issues of understanding the work of the Holy Spirit, which is also common, the main issues for sung worship not working properly are generally that congregations:

- don't love each other enough;

- don't trust each other enough;

- struggle to identify anything to be thankful for;

- are unsure about how to express themselves.

There's a real lack of synergy.

The problem is that, if those things are out of alignment, you can experience sung worship in a dysfunctional way, or completely kill it all together.

Funnily enough, if the problem is a lack of love for or trust in your church family, you could still at least experience vibrant self-centred sung worship. This isn't ideal but at least it gets things going, and it certainly looks and sounds pretty. If only that were the point!

Conversely, an issue with thankfulness or confidence is really hard to sort out, and there's really no upside to it. The issue here is a lack of joy, which kills off the creativity you need to build confidence.

Sung worship flowing from this place is basically just dead on arrival. If we go right down to the root of this, I think that being able to express thankfulness starts with understanding where you're from, and how you got to where you are today. It's about being saved and feeling the effects enough to be able to respond appropriately.

Have a think. Do you remember life before Jesus? Do you know anyone who's still full of the joy of who Jesus is?

People who can recall the moment they found Christ often look up to those who've known Jesus for their entire lives. Sadly, they often get frustrated with how monotone worship can be, which is a real shame.

I'll never forget a preacher I heard on a camp as a kid. He said something like, "If you're not excited about Jesus, please don't tell people you're a Christian!"

We laughed so much, and knew he was joking, but maybe he also had a good point. If we're not glorifying God through a lens of joy, and if we have no real appreciation for the breadth of His grace, then maybe we've not understood.

> *The ropes of death entangled me;*
> *   floods of destruction swept over me.*
> *The grave wrapped its ropes around me;*
> *   death laid a trap in my path.*
> *But in my distress I cried out to the LORD;*
> *   yes, I prayed to my God for help.*
> *He heard me from his sanctuary;*
> *   my cry to him reached his ears.*
>
> *Then the earth quaked and trembled.*
> *   The foundations of the mountains shook;*
> *   they quaked because of his anger.*
> *Smoke poured from his nostrils;*
> *   fierce flames leaped from his mouth.*
> *   Glowing coals blazed forth from him.*
> *He opened the heavens and came down;*
> *   dark storm clouds were beneath his feet.*
> *Mounted on a mighty angelic being, he flew,*
> *   soaring on the wings of the wind.*

He shrouded himself in darkness,
veiling his approach with dark rain clouds.
Thick clouds shielded the brightness
around him and rained down hail and burning coals.
The LORD thundered from heaven;
the voice of the Most High resounded
amid the hail and burning coals.
He shot his arrows and scattered his enemies;
great bolts of lightning flashed, and they were
confused.
Then at your command, O LORD,
at the blast of your breath,
the bottom of the sea could be seen,
and the foundations of the earth were laid bare.

He reached down from heaven and rescued me;
He drew me out of deep waters.
He rescued me from my powerful enemies,
from those who hated me and were too strong for me.
Psalm 18:4–17 NLT

Do you realise that before Jesus died and rose again, we were so lost that God's emotional response to how broken we were became nothing short of terrifyingly violent?

Psalm 18 paints us a great picture. The most incredible thing about this is that God is always the same, which means that even after Jesus' resurrection and ascension, He's still this guy.

I have some very mixed-up memories of what life was like when I was very young. Generally speaking I've been OK with the muddle, but as I have grown older it has become important for me to figure it out a bit. For example, I remember sitting on a bean bag or soft chair in the window of a home we moved away from just before my third birthday. But I'm not sure whether that's a real memory or not.

I also have a memory of my nana's home, mostly about sitting in her living room and kitchen. I remember a coal scoop in the living room, and I remember the kitchen was quite dark. I think there were plastic-wrapped chair backs, but I don't remember being there with anyone other than her. I do think this is mostly a proper memory. The oddest thing I remember is something I know didn't actually happen – at least, not like this.

I was perched on the arm of the sofa, swinging on the brass handle of my parents' living room door. My brother and sister were next to me, and as we sat, my dad, a couple of other people, and my step-mum walked in. As I was swinging on the door, I could hear them telling us that my mum had passed away, and I didn't think I understood it. In fact, I was not even sure I knew who they were talking about, so I carried on swinging. I might have only been three or four years old.

You see the problem. In this memory of mine, my step-mum was part of the group, but in actual fact she wasn't around yet, not until quite a while later. Fast forward to when my step-mum actually came into our lives and I remember this bit really well.

It was my dad and step-mum's wedding day, and I was being really hard to handle. I wasn't trying to be naughty; it was just so overwhelming and I desperately needed my daddy to keep close. I think there's even a picture of me hanging on his suit leg scowling at the world, while everyone else beamed with big smiles at the joy of the day. I wasn't cross about the wedding. In fact, if you see me in large social situations now, you'll see me acting in much the same way.

As we grew into a family I quickly loved calling this lady "Mum", and in time a new younger brother arrived. I thought he was great and we were really close. But as a young teenager, despite everything good that had come before, I started to get the feeling that I didn't want my new mum around.

It was odd. I had no connection with my actual mother, never visited her grave, and couldn't even remember the anniversary of her death. Yet suddenly it bothered me that I had a step-mum. I just started to find her a real annoyance. I didn't enjoy hugging her, and I didn't even want her to be helpful or loving. I just wanted to be left alone.

After a while that feeling passed, but I wasn't any the wiser about why I'd felt like that, although now I'm an adult I think I understand a bit better. In some ways what I went through was pretty normal for a teenage boy. But I was also trying to understand that there was a lady who people say I'm similar to, who loved me, and who wasn't supposed to go. And I was struggling with that at the same time as trying to understand that there was this other lady who raised me, whom I couldn't remember not being there. To me, this second lady was always my mum, and she inhabited every single memory I had.

A few years ago, I started to properly understand the fact that I had two mums, but then I struggled to figure out which one was supposed to be more important to me. After a while it became easier, and in time I figured it out. As important as my birth mum was to other people, the only mum I have is the one who won the right to be called "my mum", and I choose her, because she chose me.

My experiences here won't resonate with everyone, but there's an element you need to try to understand.

Until we're comfortable enough to outwardly proclaim that we've understood something enough to choose it, we're unlikely to be able to express any level of joy through it. Until it's chosen, it's just sort of there, doing nothing.

Think of it like this: no matter how your particular personality quirks guide you, when someone thrills your heart, you're likely to hug them.

No matter your background, when you achieve something unexpected, you're likely to share a high five or a "Yes!" moment with someone else involved.

No matter your position, you're likely to be drawn to a shared moment of quiet when a person loses someone dear to them. It would be really odd if you didn't.

You see, we respond based on our own level of understanding – and of course, an amalgamation of different experiences, thoughts, and feelings that lead us to do what we do in different situations.

And when we choose Jesus,

understanding what He saved us from,

realising what He saved us for,

looking forward to what He saved us to become,

an automatic reaction is inevitable.

It's an explosion.

It's an overflow.

It's an eruption.

You can't help it: it springs from deep within your soul.

> Let everything within me cry out, cry out;
> joining with the earth to shout out, shout out;
> worthy is the Lamb who reigns by Your side.
> I will glorify.
> I choose for my heart to always worship You,
> And I will make my soul cry out,
> "It is You that I adore."

A great mentor of mine from the States talks about how, if we love Jesus, then our "first love" needs to actually be Him. He and his wife taught Louise and me that our hearts need to be opened up before God, like David opened up his heart. It's excellent teaching, but more interesting for this illustration is how they teach it. Generally speaking, they do it in groups.

You see, although the principle of opening up your heart before God is essentially private, there's a powerful corporate application that is even better. It's quite literally an activity that ticks every box we're talking about in this chapter:

- it deepens love between the people in the group;

- it builds trust among the people in the group;

- it helps us to identify what we're thankful for;

- it builds confidence in self-expression;

- it helps us to understand the work of the Holy Spirit.

One of the best parts of the "first love" teaching is a practical activity called "heart psalms". This is a heart psalm that I wrote a couple of years back in a session with them:

> Lord, my heart before You is growing. I'm so aware that
> You're moving in the lives of people that I love and I'm
> worried that I don't have enough of what I need to give to
> them.

You are God, I am not.
Your love is wonderful, mine is not.
Your plan is perfect, mine is not.
You're a good Father,
I'm too inconsistent.
You are faithful,
I'm distracted too easily.
You are good, and your love endures forever.

When I shared this, the most amazing thing happened. The people in the group instantly empathised with me. And as they prayed for me, the Holy Spirit started to move, giving people words and pictures for me. And then after I'd finished, we heard someone else's heart psalm, and continued around the group until everyone had shared. On one occasion, this took a couple of hours, and every minute was amazing. It was just wonderful.

The purpose was to open up our hearts before God, but the activity also opened up our hearts before each other. As we reflected together, the Holy Spirit did more than we could imagine. And it was a truly wonderful time together.

As we draw to a close for this chapter, let's be really clear what we're talking about here.

First, there's a genuine need for worshippers to cultivate meaningful connections with each other. Creating excellent sounds is wonderful, but it comes a poor second to the releasing of gifts, which comes from a deep love and trust in the worship space.

Second, we'll be far more capable of expressing joy in Jesus when we've understood what we've been saved from. And to be honest, we need to understand that we're saved from our past, saved from what happened the other day, saved for today, and saved from what we could easily become if we step away from Jesus tomorrow.

Finally, we're looking for deep connection here. And so when there's an overflow of thankfulness in a group of believers who are able to open up their hearts together, you'll know you're surrounded by a group of people who love Jesus, and understand enough about His love and sacrifice, to choose to follow Him, as He chose to give Himself for us.

Movement

Take a moment to open your heart in honesty before God.

"God, my heart before You is... (describe how you feel before God), like a... (try to unpack the words you used with some descriptive language)."

CHAPTER 11

Discipline: Discipleship and the Kingdom of Heaven

It was an early autumn morning and my wife and I were late for work. It was no big deal, except that we were also struggling to get a toddler ready, which made things at least three times more difficult.

It's funny how time and circumstance can change you. When Madeline was a newborn, we would never have been caught up in a chaotic moment like this. But then, when a baby is about to be born, there are a million books to read on the subject, not to mention the NHS support and the helpful or less than helpful opinions of people who've "been through it before", so you can't really fail.

We had done as much preparation as we could in the run-up to her birth; we'd bought newborn nappies, baby grows, vests, and a full set of new furniture for a designated room we wouldn't end up using for at least two months. And then there was the changing table, cotton wool, and a couple of bowls for "essential" water. Of course, we could have installed a sink as one book suggested. Really, that book exists!

We had Sudocrem, talc, tiny baby versions of brushes, nail clippers, and of course a hundred and thirty-two thousand muslin cloths.

The day we brought Madeline home went like clockwork. We thought we were completely ready for this little person to come home. That is, we were prepared for the practicalities, but we were not expecting jaundice, nearly starving her when she wasn't feeding well, or being told we had a "naughty baby" (true story). We weren't prepared for Louise being strong-armed into continuing to breastfeed, or to me being "removed" from the conversation because men can't be trusted or something (again true). Then there was the endless screaming and crying, and finally, going in to get some good old-fashioned, proper midwife support that completely set us on the right path. I love those midwives!

Phew, the first few days at home were tough. But once we got the initial "Whoa!" sorted out, we became a well-oiled machine. The daytimes were pretty great, and we filled our time with figuring out how to be parents. But, when the sun went down, we did our really impressive work.

We called it "the nighttime reset". The aim was to make the next day run mega smoothly from the off. This is basically how it worked.

At around 7 p.m., we'd finish an evening feed, clear up from dinner, and settle in. Then we'd enjoy the evening and watch a movie or something.

At about 11 p.m., Louise would get on with the next feed and I'd get us ready to go to bed. I'd also put on a wash.

Then at around 2 a.m., we'd wake up and spring into full-blown ninja action.

Louise got the baby up while I warmed up the bottle; then, when the bottle was ready, and the baby was feeding, it was all systems go:

- unload the washing;

- put on another load;

- put everything out to dry;

- make Louise some toast and a drink while she fed the baby;

- sterilise bottles;

- sterilise surfaces;

- sterilise every tiny molecule in the cottage;

- do the washing up and sterilise the surfaces again.

Finally, we'd go back to bed. It was just incredible. Louise was incredible; I was incredible! And we went on and on doing this until one night when Madeline slept right through. And that was it. Baby slept better. Parents lost the plot.

The problem we had was that as Madeline slept better, she became more inconsistent: a whole night, half a night, waking up four times a night, and sleeping far too long. And that was it – the end of the most disciplined time of our entire lives.

This is precisely the issue with trying to be disciplined. We start a thing, then tiredness takes over and we stop. We start a diet, and a birthday comes along so we fill our faces, get discouraged, and stop. We want to be fit, but we don't see change quickly enough, so we stop. Something changes, and we stop.

You see, the problem we have is that life is so full of change. Finding some discipline within the most conducive times is fine, but as time moves on, we're not likely to give the opportunity for what we're trying to establish to become consistent. Sometimes the thing we're most focused on isn't even worth the effort in the first place.

However, real, meaningful, lifelong discipline isn't founded on the whims or goals of the moment. It's more about figuring out a purpose, which then needs to be followed up by some carefully considered actions. In some ways, it should be easy for us to establish what this is all about. Let's remember what we covered in previous chapters:

- Chapter 7: The purpose of choice

- Chapter 8: The purpose of being present

- Chapter 9: The purpose of exercising grace

- Chapter 10: The purpose of thankfulness

And here we are in Chapter 11, talking about the purpose of discipline.

Do you know, it's a bit of a pain for this chapter, but Jesus never actually talked about discipline? Instead, He almost exclusively talked about bringing the kingdom of heaven here.

Why is that, do you think? Did He forget? Maybe He just isn't big on personal development principles? Conversely, James, Peter, John, and Paul were obsessed by it. I think Paul nailed it best.

> Don't you realise that in a race everyone runs, but only one person gets the prize? So run to win! All athletes are disciplined in their training. They do it to win a prize that will fade away, but we do it for an eternal prize. So I run with purpose in every step. I am not just shadowboxing. I discipline my body like an athlete, training it to do what it should. Otherwise, I fear that after preaching to others I

> *myself might be disqualified.*
> **1 Corinthians 9:24–27 NLT**

Of course, Jesus may not have taught explicitly on it, but discipline was centrally important to Him, and unsurprisingly He led a highly disciplined lifestyle.

Interestingly though, when Jesus is disciplined, it looks and feels like a key to opening up heavenly moments; whereas, when the lads teach about discipline, it seems more like:

"OK, everyone, Jesus has gone, and it turns out this stuff is really super hard, so here are some thoughts on not being a complete failure."

Let's just pause a moment and make sure we're on the same page.

Highly disciplined doesn't equal sinless,

although Jesus was without sin.

Highly disciplined doesn't mean becoming perfect,

although again, Jesus was perfect.

Highly disciplined doesn't mean always being right.

You see where I'm going with this?

Living a highly disciplined lifestyle doesn't mean you won't also be fun, relaxed or crazy at times. And it doesn't mean that you become boring or immovable either.

Living a highly disciplined lifestyle should actually mean that you're moving "towards" something – not that you'll get it right all the time, but that you're moving nonetheless. We should be moving towards:

- being certain of who we are;

- being certain of our surroundings;

- being certain of what gives us life;

- being certain of what helps us grow;

- being certain of what our calling is;

- being certain of what our mission is.

Why is being certain so important? Well, being certain is what comes after you've chosen, but before you've achieved anything. It means I've understood it enough to choose it, and now:

I'm going to live a life that's committed to it.

It's one big, "No, I will not give up."

I won't let mistakes faze me,

I will run this race as if I mean to win.

I won't compare myself to anyone else.

I will win the prize for which Christ has called me heavenward.

Is that the prize for the No. 1 most disciplined human? No, thankfully not. Discipline is supposed to be an invitation for everyone to see God's kingdom come. We turn ourselves slowly and surely towards Him, and let the Holy Spirit transform us into who He's called us to be. This process is so special, and it's deeply rooted in Jesus' power.

He's the spoken Word at creation,

the justice of the Father,

the one who draws us closer.

He frees us from sin,

He bought us with His blood,

He cleans us off,

He presents us as holy before God.

Never forget that there's a you-shaped mark on the Father. Never forget that you're His great treasure.

And this is where we land. As I write this, I'm looking out on a warm spring day. I've just finished turning our old king-sized bed frame into a garden bench for the family, and there's a little breeze in the air. It's subtle, but even the evergreens at the bottom of my garden are swaying a bit.

Do you know that you're designed to thrive on days like these? You're designed to sway to the movement of His Spirit. And honestly, you can push and push and train and strain all you like, but real change takes ages, and even the most disciplined of individuals will only change a little at a time. You see:

- your body is designed for slow change;

- your heart is designed for slow chang;

- your mind is designed for slow change;

- your spirit is designed for slow change;

- it takes understanding of purpose;

- it takes being certain;

- it takes resolve, but it's not supposed to hurt.

It's supposed to look like a lifelong daily walk in the right direction. And when we move in the direction of God's heart in different situations, the kingdom of heaven is revealed.

Keep in mind, God carries us out of winter, but we really need to be planning to walk with Him in the spring. And so we pray, we worship, we study, we fast, and we practise being quiet in private spaces. We make sure we sleep a good amount, eat right, keep fit, guard our relationships, mind we don't gossip, keep a well-ordered home ready for company, and so on.

And it's all so that we're in tune. Not filling our lives with busyness, but valuing the basics, and responding to people around us in love, bringing God's kingdom here.

There's a primary school assembly I do called "pencil windmills". In the assembly, I help a child turn a pencil into a windmill. It's basically a Pentecost assembly, and it's really fun.

At the end, I explain that we're all fitted with a spiritual windmill – every single one of us. So when we experience the Holy Spirit move, we'll respond, gently moving closer to Jesus in the breeze of His presence.

We can even feel the effects in relationships, in compliments, in perfect moments of love and grace, in disappointment, in hardship, and in grief. And it shouldn't surprise us at all that God would be present in all of those situations. God is always present.

Don't ever be fooled. If you love Jesus, the greatest reason to be more disciplined is to see His kingdom come. Of course, living a more disciplined life will vastly improve everything else about you, but if your purpose in living a disciplined life is simply to achieve more, or look better, then you've missed something important in the detail: DISCIPLESHIP. And that is really what we're talking about in this chapter, and indeed the entire book.

If we love Him, we'll put His words into practice.

If we love Him, we'll be like wise builders and build on a rock.

If we love Him, we'll comply with what He taught us to do.

You'd better check out Matthew 5–7 yourself, or we'll be here all day, but if you want to see His kingdom come, you'll learn to accept the need to love and practise discipline.

Movement

Take a moment to open your heart in honesty before God.

What do you sense God is saying to you? Where do you sense He's leading you?

CHAPTER 12

Freedom: Hope and Restoration

My dad found it really hard to make plans. In between his lifelong need for naps, he struggled to fit in things that needed doing in the "every day", let alone having the headspace to consider something that someone else thought might be fun or important. I think that made him kind of selfish at times, but he wasn't malicious; he had just struggled with various forms of illness his entire life and always had to work around that.

When my dad was younger, we shared some really amazing, funny times together. Of course these might seem dumb to you, but to me they're such wonderful memories. Like this one time when my dad and I put socks on our ears and danced around the house. Sounds silly... but it was comedy gold!

There was another time when we blasted Cliff Richard's *Wired for Sound* out of the speakers of his old car. I even remember standing in the footwell between the two front seats of the car (before seatbelt laws came in) talking to him, and messing around with his hair.

For most of my life, Dad worked complicated shift patterns, but on the evenings he was home, he and I would play board games together, and when he had the time he would teach me how to print photos the old-fashioned way in his loft office.

One year he promised me a movie birthday party. Michael Jackson's *Moonwalker* had come to VHS, but we didn't have a video player. As the story goes, he organised to hire the movie and the video player, but when it came time to pick them up the shop was closed, so instead of coming home empty-handed, he came back with a new VHS video player of our very own.

Those times were the best. One of my absolute favourite memories was of a day when he promised me a copy of his cassette tape: *ABBA, The Visitors*. I think I'd pestered him for ages, but he wasn't keen on making quick decisions. When he did finally agree, he got a blank cassette tape and took me into the living room to make the copy. These days, if you want a copy of something you download it or do a file transfer from your smartphone or computer, but back in those days if you were to copy music, you had to do it in real time using a double cassette deck.

I can still picture the scene – Dad sitting by the fireplace next to the tape recorder, and me hanging over the arm of the chair. He put the ABBA tape in one side of the recorder, and I put the blank tape in the other.

The way it worked was by pressing down "play" and "record" on the one side and "play" on the other, but on this particular high-quality double tape deck, there was also a mic record button, which overrode everything. Whether we got the tapes mixed up, I don't remember, but thirty seconds into the first track, I turned to him and said, "Are you sure this is recording Daddy? That record button isn't pushed down!"

He replied, "I don't know; I don't think that's the right one."

At this point in the song we were getting to a line that said something like "Through the door, I feel I'm…", but at that moment my dad let curiosity and the seed of doubt I'd sewn get the better of him. In a moment of madness, he pressed down the extra mic "record" button, and the system overrode the standard recording process and switched seamlessly to a microphone record mode. In theory this should have been fine. We didn't want to record anything from the mic, but if it had recorded on the blank tape, we could have sorted it; however, for some reason it began to record on to the pre-recorded ABBA album.

In the moments that followed, the double deck continued to record, except the sound had disappeared entirely. We both sat in stunned silence, and then something must have clicked in my dad's brain, and he exclaimed with a loud, "Idiot!", before turning the whole thing off.

We both sat there as the tension mounted, and my dad was clearly cross as he rewound the precious ABBA tape to listen back to what he'd just done. I asked him what was happening, but as he pressed "play" and the song started again, it became hilariously apparent that something had gone very wrong.

The intro played.

The first verse started.

The pre-chorus hyped up…

And then the chorus began and got all the way to the mid-section before the audio cut out, leaving around ten seconds of silence, followed by a cross-sounding "Idiot!" from the mouth of my dad resounding in the audio.

Needless to say, I did not get my ABBA recording that day.

To this day, I'm still not sure whether he was more cross with himself or me. But there's a connection with this tape that I love, and a memory that I'll always hold dear.

This might not be immediately apparent from the story, but it's the subject of "connection" that I'd like us to finish talking about in this book – connection and its relationship with freedom.

The issue here is that when we get a taste of freedom, it's all too easy to disconnect for a while in favour of feeling the fresh air. We adopt an independence that we sense we deserve. But when we're running from what got us stuck in the first place, we've got to understand that we're running towards something else.

When you're a kid, everything is pretty straightforward. If something goes wrong, you can look at it as bad, get an adult to sort it out, and then run towards anything good. However, when we're thinking about the more complicated problems that come with adulthood, merely turning away from the bad thing is more problematic than it might first seem.

If we get it wrong, we can end up turning away from being stuck in one way, to reaching out for something we think is better, only to find that it's just another place to get stuck. For example, if you've been put down your whole life, getting unstuck from that might look like grabbing hold of your own self-confidence and worth, but it's so important not to become self-centred or jaded in the process.

Let's open this up a bit more.

For all the research undertaken, the newest thinking shows that when you're getting unstuck from addiction, it isn't helpful to isolate yourself. If you're struggling with addiction, you need a positive, life-affirming community to surround you.

How about intolerance? We teach people that we need to turn away from intolerance to become more tolerant, but tolerance is defined as being willing to put up with differences in others, and I'm not so sure this is correct. If I'm merely tolerating something about you, your beliefs or lifestyle, I'm still somehow acting as if I'm sitting above you. But we need to go further towards the way Jesus teaches us to find deep, genuine love and grace for each other.

In the same way, when we're looking to get unstuck from whatever it is we're struggling with, the answer isn't simply to become "free", independently expressing the freedom in whatever way we feel we need. The response to, and the opposite of being "stuck in the mud", has to be to connect or reconnect with the author of your life. We need to get unstuck and get plugged right into the never-ending stream of life, which comes from Jesus.

> *"I am the true grapevine, and my Father is the gardener. He cuts off every branch of mine that doesn't produce fruit, and he prunes the branches that do bear fruit so they will produce even more. You have already been pruned and purified by the message I have given you. Remain in me, and I will remain in you. For a branch cannot produce fruit if it is severed from the vine, and you cannot be fruitful unless you remain in me.*
>
> *"Yes, I am the vine; you are the branches. Those who remain in me, and I in them, will produce much fruit. For apart from me you can do nothing. Anyone who does not remain in me is thrown away like a useless branch and withers. Such branches are gathered into a pile to be burned. But if you remain in me and my words remain in you, you may ask for anything you want, and it will be granted! When you produce much fruit, you are my true disciples. This brings great glory to my Father.*
>
> *"I have loved you even as the Father has loved me. Remain in my love. When you obey my commandments, you remain in my love, just as I obey my Father's commandments and remain in his love. I have told you these things so that you will be filled with my joy. Yes, your joy will overflow! This is my commandment: Love each other in the same way I have loved you. There is no greater love than to lay down one's life for one's friends. You are my friends if you do what I command. I no longer call you slaves, because a master doesn't confide in his*

> *slaves. Now you are my friends, since I have told you*
> *everything the Father told me. You didn't choose me. I*
> *chose you. I appointed you to go and produce lasting*
> *fruit, so that the Father will give you whatever you ask for,*
> *using my name. This is my command: Love each other."*
> **John 15:1–17 NLT**

Last summer, I found myself clearing a large area of our garden. It's an area I've been working on for about five years. It started out as two trees, two sheds, and a whole lot of weeds, but as the years have gone on, I've had the ambition to get in control of the entire area. The problem is that it's far too big a job for one person to deal with in one go.

First of all, I got rid of one of the trees and one of the sheds. That was hard enough, but when I went back to do more work on the area the following season, I found that the tree had regrown enough to be a massive problem again. And where the shed had been, a delicious but very annoying blackberry bush had wholly taken over, leading to another mass of work.

As the years have gone on, I've quite literally dealt with one problem, only to find another couple of issues have cropped up in their place. As someone who likes to solve a problem and move on, I find it so frustrating that I have to continually resolve the issues in the garden.

Of course, the problem here is that I thought the opposite of an untidy garden was a garden that could be sorted in one challenging but fulfilling project. However, what I've discovered is that the answer to a messy garden is a garden that I'm connected to with a much deeper commitment – a garden I'm plugged into.

In John 15, Jesus talks about being linked to Him. We know Jesus really well as a shepherd, but in this picture, he's more of an award-winning gardener, and like any good gardener, He's continually looking to improve things. This process is painstaking for the gardener and the garden, but it's all essential.

Let me repeat this: I think we often spend so long stuck in our issues that, when the feeling of freedom comes, we can end up acting like it means being disconnected altogether. But freedom from being stuck only means something when we're released from the mud we're in, and plug ourselves into the vine – into Jesus.

How sad, if we were to get to the end of this whole journey, only to realise that our own independence was just another place we were getting ourselves stuck. Let's go over this one more time:

- real freedom comes when we understand our identity;
- real freedom grows in our love for God and each other;
- real freedom is found through leaving a legacy of love, hope, acceptance, and peace in others;
- real freedom is discovered when we join with God's heart in worship;
- real freedom is surrendering to Jesus' peace;
- real freedom is accepting God's sovereignty;
- real freedom is doing what we're called to do;
- real freedom settles your heart to be more present;
- real freedom releases you to exercise grace over others;
- real freedom is located in the fullness that comes from remaining connected with Jesus Himself.

I'm afraid that when it comes to freedom, we're going to have to accept our connection with Jesus. Sometimes we'll do well and bear fruit, and sometimes we won't. Sometimes we'll get stuck in the same issues over and over again, and we'll need the people around us to love us through.

But if we accept that being connected with Jesus is essential for our growth, then we'll find real freedom from guilt, real freedom from shame, and real freedom to discover the kind of fullness that Jesus promises is available to you today, for the rest of your life into eternity.

Movement

Earlier in the book we talked about how much Jesus understands our struggles.

Spend a moment now allowing God to speak to you. If something is causing you pain or shame, you might really need His loving arms around you.

And Finally...

We're God's great treasure. We come alive when we express love for Him, and each other. We have a responsibility to leave love as our legacy. And if we want to see God's presence impact the world, we need to choose to adore Jesus, allowing His peace to define us.

And we have to be practical. We simply won't succeed unless we get our everyday lives right.

As we come to a close, my prayer for you is that you're experiencing genuine release from whatever you've been stuck in.

> May the God of restoration reach down and draw you
> into a place of safety.
> And may you always find Him.
> Amen.